FACTS AT YOUR
FINGERTIPS

BIRDS

BROWN
BEAR
BOOKS

Published by Brown Bear Books Limited

An imprint of
The Brown Reference Group plc
68 Topstone Road
Redding
Connecticut
06896
USA
www.brownreference.com

ISBN-10: 1-933834-00-5
ISBN-13: 978-1-93383-400-9

Authors: David Chandler, Dominic Couzens, Euan Dunn, Jonathan Elphick, Rob Hume, Derek Niemann, Tony Whitehead, John Woodward

Editorial Director: Lindsey Lowe

Project Director: Graham Bateman

Art Director: Steve McCurdy

Editor: Virginia Carter

Artists: Denys Ovenden, Norman Arlott, Ad Cameron, with Trevor Boyer, Robert Gillmor, Peter Harrison, Sean Milne, Ian Willis

Printed in USA

Jacket artwork: Front: Trevor Boyer (Top Left); Ad Cameron (Center, Right).
Reverse: Ad Cameron.

Contents

Introduction

Birds are masters of the air. The only other major group of animals that has conquered the problems of flight is the insects. The oldest-known fossil that resembles a bird is *Archaeopteryx* and dates back some 150 million years. It was a dinosaurlike creature the size of a pigeon and was half-bird, half-reptile. Later true bird fossils belonging to various lineages were found in Cretaceous deposits. By the close of the Cretaceous, 65 million years ago, a hypothetical birdwatcher would have seen relatives of many of the familiar birds of today, such as geese, ducks, and shorebirds. By the early Oligocene, 35 million years ago, most of the bird orders that we recognize today had appeared—our birdwatcher could add herons, penguins, crows, vultures, songbirds, and many more to his or her list.

Today there are about 9,845 species of birds alive. They range in size from the tiny bee hummingbird, *Mellisuga helenae*, which is not much bigger than a large insect, to heavyweights like the ostrich, *Struthio camelus*. At 330 pounds (150 kg) it is the heaviest bird and stands taller than a fully grown man. The biggest-known bird (now extinct) was the ostrichlike giant moa, *Dinornis maximus*, which grew to a height of over 10 feet (3 m).

What Makes a Bird?

A simple definition could be that birds are "warm-blooded" (more properly called endothermic) vertebrates (animals with backbones) that are typically adapted to flight and that reproduce by laying eggs, which are then incubated. Birds walk on their hind limbs; the forelimbs are adapted as wings, even in species that cannot fly. A bird has a horny sheath on its jaws that forms the bill (or beak). And most distinctively, a bird has feathers covering most of its body. While some other vertebrates can fly (such as bats) and a few fish, frogs, and reptiles can glide, no creature matches the bird for sheer aerial ability. Flight has enabled birds to colonize distant lands, invade new habitats, and find food over vast distances. It has also given them a means of escaping from land-bound enemies.

During the course of evolution a few species have lost the ability to fly. Large flightless birds such as the ostrich, *Struthio camelus*, and the emu, *Dromaius novaehollandiae*, overcome this drawback by their great size and strength and the ability to outrun their enemies. The wings of penguins have evolved to become powerful flippers for propelling them through water instead of through the air.

A bird's skeleton is highly adapted to its flying lifestyle. Most significantly, bones are light to reduce weight, and the breastbone has a deep keel providing anchorage for the large flight muscles that drive the wings. Bird feathers come in three main types: Flight feathers are large and found on the wings and tail. They provide the lift and guidance system for a bird in flight. Contour feathers give the bird its streamlined form over much of its body. Finally, the soft down feathers form insulating layers. Feathers, of course, give each species its distinctive color and pattern.

About this Book

Just by looking, we can see that all terns and gulls are probably related and that herons and storks are quite different from penguins. Scientists take this study much further and to minute detail in the science of taxonomy, in which detailed relationships are worked out using a hierarchy of categories called taxa. Birds all belong to the class Aves, which is divided into 28 orders. Examples include the order Charadriiformes (gulls, terns, and shorebirds), Sphenisciformes (penguins), and Ciconiiformes (storks and herons). In *Facts at Your Fingertips: Birds* you will find representatives of most bird orders, which are color coded. Within an order such as

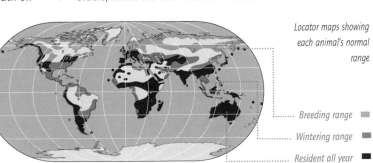

Locator maps showing each animal's normal range

Breeding range ■
Wintering range ■
Resident all year ■

Charadriiformes, all gull-like birds are placed in the family Laridae, while ternlike birds are in the family Sternidae. There are about 172 families of birds in total. Very closely related terns, such as the common tern and Caspian tern are placed in the genus *Sterna*. Finally, common and Caspian terns are distinguished by the scientific names *Sterna hirundo* and *Sterna caspia* respectively. In this book you will find illustrated entries on 112 species of bird, grouped by order and family.

Each entry follows a fixed structure. The color-coded header strip denotes the order or related groups of orders to which each bird belongs, and gives its common name. The fact panel then lists its scientific name and other taxonomic information followed by sections that describe different features of the animal and its lifestyle. Like all animals, the survival of many birds is in doubt as they suffer from man-made pressures. Under the heading "Status" information is given on the threats or lack of threat facing each animal. For definitions of the categories of threat see Glossary under IUCN and CITES.
Finally, a world map visually portrays the distribution of each species, showing its natural range unless otherwise indicated *(see left for key).*

The kingdom Animalia is subdivided into phyla, classes, orders, families, genera, and species. Below is the classification of the Caspian tern.

Rank	Scientific name	Common name
Phylum	Chordata	Animals with a backbone
Class	Aves	All birds
Order	Charadriiformes	Gulls and their relatives
Family	Sternidae	Terns
Genus	*Sterna*	Sea terns
Species	*caspia*	Caspian tern

Common Pheasant

Peregrine Falcon

Wood Stork

Black-Capped Chickadee

Toucan Barbet

Examples of the major groups of birds.

Emperor Penguin

Belted Kingfisher

Ostrich

Common name Ostrich

Scientific name *Struthio camelus*

Family Struthionidae

Order Struthioniformes

Size Height: male 83–108 in (210–275 cm), female 69–75 in (175–190 cm); weight: male 287–331 lb (130–150 kg), female 198–243 lb (90–110 kg)

Key features Bare head, neck, and legs; short, flat bill; large, dark eyes; male black with short, white wings and tail; female dull gray-brown

Habits Lives in small groups or flocks, feeding by day

Nesting Nest a scrape in the ground; usually 7 eggs; male and dominant female incubate eggs, including many laid by other females; chicks gather in large congregations, several families looked after by 1 pair of adults; young fully grown at 18 months; mature at 3–4 years; 1 brood

Voice Variety of short, hard calls, sneezing sounds, and a loud, deep, roaring or booming sound from territorial male

Diet Succulent plants, leaves, buds, seeds, fruits; rarely insects, small mammals, and reptiles

Habitat Open spaces from semiarid areas on desert edge to clearings in savanna woodland; mostly on open, grassy plains

Distribution Africa south of the Sahara Desert

Status Rare and threatened in the north and south of its range; secure in East Africa; some escaped populations from farmed stock in southern Africa

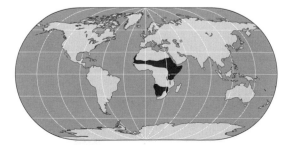

Emu

Common name Emu

Scientific name *Dromaius novaehollandiae*

Family Dromaiidae

Order Casuariiformes

Size Height: 59–75 in (150–190 cm); weight: 66–121 lb (30–55 kg)

Key features Bulky, horizontal body with bushy brown feathers; vestigial wings and tail; heavily feathered lower neck, male has bare blue-gray upper neck; female has black upper neck and blue face; rather deep, pointed bill; long, brown legs

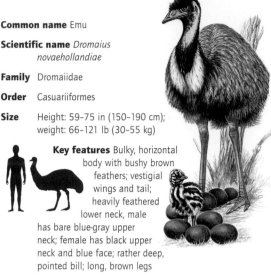

Habits Feeds during daylight, singly or in groups; usually seeks shade in hottest part of the day; roosts on the ground

Nesting Nest is a hollow on the ground; 5–15 eggs; incubation by the male for 56 days; chicks cared for by male and become mature at 2–3 years; 1 brood

Voice Usually silent, but some grunting and booming calls in breeding season

Diet Seeds, fruits, flowers, roots; also large insects

Habitat Open forest and semiarid plains; occasionally desert areas or suburban open spaces

Distribution Widespread in Australia

Status Stable; locally increasing

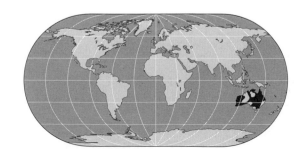

Common Rhea

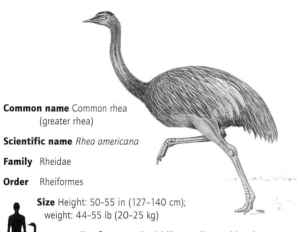

Common name Common rhea
(greater rhea)

Scientific name *Rhea americana*

Family Rheidae

Order Rheiformes

Size Height: 50–55 in (127–140 cm);
weight: 44–55 lb (20–25 kg)

Key features Ostrichlike; small, round head
and broad, flat bill on upright, slender,
feathered neck; round body with bushy brown
plumage; black chest; long, powerful, gray-
brown legs

Habits Gregarious, living on bushy plains; long-striding; diurnal

Nesting Male makes nest and fights for females, which lay eggs
in it as a group before leaving to mate with other males;
incubation by male for 30–35 days; young mature at
2–3 years; 1 brood

Voice Deep, far-carrying, double roar or grunt; also produces
whistling calls

Diet Mostly vegetable matter; also some insects, amphibians,
reptiles, and small mammals

Habitat Grasslands such as the Brazilian campo and the
Argentinian pampas

Distribution South-central Brazil southward through Uruguay,
Paraguay, and Argentina

Status Declining, near-threatened

Brown Kiwi

Common name Brown kiwi

Scientific name *Apteryx australis*

Family Apterygidae

Order Apterygiformes

Size Length: 19.5–25.5 in (50–65 cm);
weight: 3–8 lb (1.4–3.6 kg)

Key features Pear-shaped, terrestrial bird with long, thin bill
and round head; no tail; stumpy legs; dense, dark
brown plumage

Habits Feeds at night; spends daytime in burrows

Nesting Nests in burrow or cavity; up to 3 eggs; incubation
75–84 days by the male; chicks independent after
14–20 days; young males mature at 14 months, and
females mature at 2 years; 1 brood

Voice Shrill, far-carrying whistles that rise and fall in pitch; also
grunts and growls

Diet Mostly invertebrates; some seeds and leaves

Habitat Dense rain forest; now forced to occupy scrub, thickets,
and grassland edge in absence of true habitat

Distribution Very local on both North and South Island
of New Zealand and various offshore islands

Status Declining, but not yet threatened

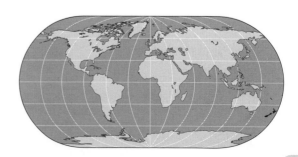

Northern Bobwhite

Common name Northern bobwhite (bobwhite)

Scientific name *Colinus virginianus*

Family Phasianidae

Order Galliformes

Size Length: 8–10 in (20–25 cm); wingspan: 17 in (43 cm); weight: 4 oz (113 g)

Key features Small, rounded, rusty-brown quail with tiny bill; males have very variable head pattern—according to race—from all-black to blackish, with buff or white stripe over eye and on throat; both sexes unmarked or spotted white below; females generally duller

Habits Ground-dwelling; found in small family parties

Nesting Shallow nest on ground; 10–15 eggs; incubation 23 days; young fledge after 14 days; 1 brood

Voice Clear, whistled "bob-white!" and "kal-oi-kee?"

Diet Seeds and fruits; insects in summer

Habitat Open woodland, woodland edge and shrubbery, arable fields, pastures, and open grassland

Distribution Eastern U.S. south into Central America; also Cuba

Status Abundant; more than 20 million shot annually in U.S.

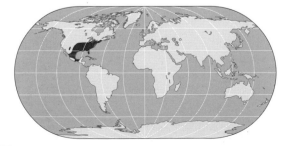

Indian Peafowl

Common name Indian peafowl (blue peafowl, peacock)

Scientific name *Pavo cristatus*

Family Phasianidae

Order Galliformes

Size Length: male 71–91 in (180–231 cm), female 35–39 in (90–100 cm); wingspan: 31.5–51 in (80–130 cm); weight: 6–13.2 lb (2.7–6 kg)

Key features Male long-legged and long-necked; deep-blue plumage with rufous wingtips and barred gray coverts; enormous "eyed" train; female duller—gray-brown above, belly white; tail short and broad

Habits Forages on ground but roosts and perches freely in trees; solitary or in small groups

Nesting Nests on or near ground; 3–6 eggs; incubation by female for 28–30 days; young fledge after 21–28 days; 1 brood

Voice Loud, nasal clanging or trumpeting sound and short, braying sound from male; also "kok-kok" alarm call

Diet Seeds, grain, buds, and berries; also insects, small reptiles, and rodents

Habitat Open forest, orchards, and cultivation

Distribution Throughout India, parts of Pakistan, and Sri Lanka

Status Secure but locally scarce; in some areas still common and thriving

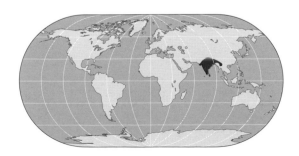

Common Pheasant

Common name Common pheasant (pheasant, ring-necked pheasant)

Scientific name *Phasianus colchicus*

Family Phasianidae

Order Galliformes

Size Length: male 29.5–35 in (75–89 cm), female 21–24.5 in (53–62 cm); wingspan: 27.5–36 in (70–91.5 cm); weight: 1.3–4.4 lb (0.6–2 kg)

Key features Round-bodied, triangular-tailed, small-headed game bird; male with green head, coppery or golden-brown body with dark spots, green to orange-buff rump; female dull, spotted, shorter-tailed

Habits Lives socially; terrestrial except when roosting; noisy at dusk

Nesting Males mate with several hens; small nest on ground; 9–14 eggs; incubation 22 days; young fledge after 12 days; 1 brood

Voice Loud, crowing calls and abrupt "korr-kok"

Diet Fruits, seeds, and buds; occasionally insects and small reptiles, amphibians, and mammals

Habitat Woodland edge, overgrown riversides, edges of marshes, and farmland

Distribution Natural range across Central and eastern Asia, west to eastern Europe; introduced widely in other parts of Europe, North America, and Australasia

Status Common and secure in original range

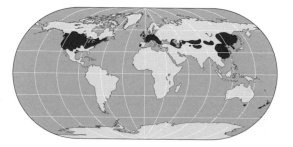

Sage Grouse

Common name Sage grouse

Scientific name *Centrocercus urophasianus*

Family Tetraonidae

Order Galliformes

Size Length: male 26–30 in (66–76 cm), female 19–23 in (48–58 cm); wingspan: 47 in (119 cm); weight: 3–7 lb (1.4–3.2 kg)

Key features Rather long, long-tailed grouse; short, dark bill; yellow wattle over eye; thickset head and neck; reddish-brown plumage with complex pattern; male black-and-white on head and neck, white ruff on breast, black plumage on belly; short legs

Habits Terrestrial; lives in small groups; males mostly separate from hens

Nesting Males display communally at leks; females nest on ground; 7–8 eggs; incubation 25–27 days; young fledge after 14–21 days; 1 brood

Voice Short, chickenlike, clucking calls when flushed

Diet Shoots and leaves of sagebrush, clover, and various herbaceous plants; young chicks require insects

Habitat Low, thick scrub and brush country, and dry grassland in plains and foothills

Distribution Widespread in western U.S and southwest Canada; range shrinking at edges

Status Locally common and secure; declining at fringe of range

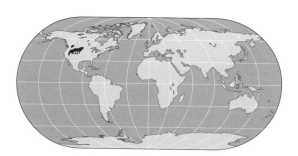

Common Turkey

Mallee Fowl

Common name
Common turkey (wild turkey)

Scientific name *Meleagris gallopavo*

Family Meleagrididae

Order Galliformes

Size Length: male 43 in (110 cm), female 36 in (91 cm); weight: 9–22 lb (4–10 kg)

Key features Massive; fairly long-tailed and long-legged; fairly upright stance; slim, bare neck; small, bare head; glossy, blackish plumage; red coloration on head (females bluish); red legs

Habits Lives in groups on the ground by day; flies up to roost in trees at night

Nesting Nest on ground; 10–13 eggs; incubation 28 days by female; young fledge after 14–21 days; 1 brood

Voice Gobbling sound made by male

Diet Acorns, seeds, fruits, leaves, shoots, and roots; young eat insects

Habitat Bushy grassland and cultivated ground near forests; temperate regions south to subtropics

Distribution Widespread in North America from Pacific to Atlantic coasts, north to Ontario and south to Florida and Mexico

Status Recent increase after long decline, now numerous; often restocked and reintroduced into parts of range from which it had been lost

Common name
Mallee fowl

Scientific name *Leipoa ocellata*

Family Megapodiidae

Order Galliformes

Size Length: 23.5 in (60 cm); wingspan: 55 in (140 cm); weight: 3.3–4.4 lb (1.5–2 kg);

Key features Round-headed, short-necked, heavy-bodied ground bird; hump-backed and short-legged; gray head and neck; thin, black head crest; short, downcurved bill; black line down middle of the foreneck and chest; white underside; barred black, brown, and cream back and wings; strong, pale gray legs with thick toes

Habits Generally solitary or in pairs; moves slowly and quietly through bushy areas and woodland; roosts in trees

Nesting Extraordinary mound built for the eggs; 15–24 eggs; incubation 62–64 days; young fledge after 24 hours; 1 brood

Voice Deep, triple booming note from male; also harsh, crowing call

Diet Mostly seeds; also berries, shoots, and leaves

Habitat Woodland and bushy areas with thick canopy above bushy ground layer

Distribution Southwestern, southern, and southeastern Australia

Status Small numbers; declining and classified as Vulnerable

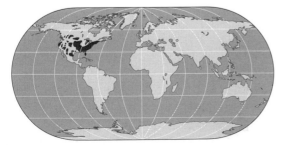

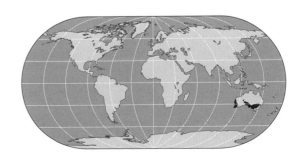

Emperor Penguin

Common name Emperor penguin

Scientific name *Aptenodytes forsteri*

Family Spheniscidae

Order Sphenisciformes

Size Length: 43–51 in (109–130 cm); flipper length: 12–16 in (30.5–41 cm); weight: 42–101 lb (19–46 kg)

Key features Very large penguin; black head, throat, and chin; large yellow ear patch not surrounded fully by dark feathers as in king penguin

Habits Lives mainly at sea, feeding by deep diving; rests on sea ice; breeds in large colonies on ice or snow

Nesting Single egg laid onto ice and transferred to male's feet for incubation for over 60 days while females leave for open ocean to feed; young fledge after about 150 days; 1 brood

Voice Loud, trumpeting contact calls; complex, rhythmic display calls; harsh threat calls

Diet Mainly fish, small squid, and krill

Habitat Breeds on sea ice or hard snow over glaciers (except for two colonies far inland that breed on packed snow over a shingle spit and on a low, rocky headland); mostly at sea off Antarctica outside breeding season

Distribution Almost entirely Antarctic within the pack ice, usually avoiding the open sea beyond

Status Up to 200,000 pairs breed; population stable overall, with some local fluctuations

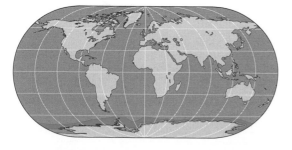

Rockhopper Penguin

Common name Rockhopper penguin (crested penguin, Victoria penguin)

Scientific name *Eudyptes chrysocome*

Family Spheniscidae

Order Sphenisciformes

Size Length: 18–23 in (46–58 cm); flipper length: 6–7.5 in (15–19 cm); weight: 4.5–7 lb (2–3.2 kg)

Key features
Medium-sized penguin; slate-gray upper parts and white underparts; short, spiky black crest that can be erected; narrow yellow stripe beginning behind base of small, stout orange-brown bill extending above red eyes to form long, drooping slender plumes projecting sideways behind each eye

Habits Gregarious at sea and on land; feeds at sea; breeds in huge, noisy colonies

Nesting Between August and March; later in southern populations; 2 white eggs laid in nest hollow, usually only 1 egg hatches; incubation by both sexes for 32–38 days; young fledge after 70 days; 1 brood

Voice Loud, harsh, pulsating braying sounds during courtship displays; grunting threat calls; also hissing, growling and squawking; barking contact calls at sea

Diet Mainly krill; also other crustaceans, small fish, squid, and octopuses

Habitat Nests on rugged rocky ground mostly near sea; feeds and winters in offshore waters

Distribution Southern Atlantic, Indian, and Pacific Oceans from southern temperate zone south to subantarctic waters

Status Recently classified as Vulnerable

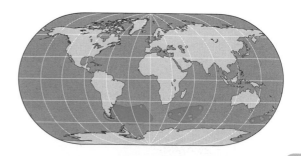

Wandering Albatross

Northern Fulmar

Common name Wandering albatross

Scientific name *Diomedea exulans*

Family Diomedeidae

Order Procellariiformes

Size Length: 43–53 in (109–135 cm); wingspan: 106–136 in (269–345 cm); weight: 14–25 lb (6.4–11.3 kg)

Key features Huge, heavy-bodied seabird; very long, narrow wings; short tail; powerful hooked bill; large webbed feet; juveniles dark brown apart from white face and mainly white underwing; plumage becomes whiter with age, with broad black to wing edges

Habits Most of year lives alone in the air, traveling across oceans and feeding at sea, but forms flocks at concentrations of food; gregarious on breeding islands

Nesting Breeds once every 2 years; generally mates for life; large, cone-shaped nest of compacted grass; 1 reddish-flecked white egg; incubation 75–83 days; young fledge after 260–303 days; 1 brood every 2 years

Voice Usually silent at sea, but croaking or bleating sounds when fighting over food; loud, hoarse braying whistles during courtship displays

Diet Mainly squid and cuttlefish; also fish, carrion, offal, and jellyfish

Habitat Breeds on remote islands, often among clumps of grass; otherwise soars over oceans

Distribution Ranges the Southern Ocean; breeding adults stay near subantarctic islands

Status Classified as Vulnerable by IUCN; total world population estimated to be fewer than 8,500 breeding pairs

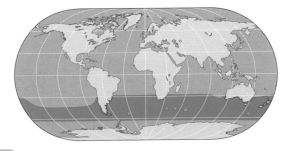

Common name Northern fulmar

Scientific name *Fulmarus glacialis*

Family Procellariidae

Order Procellariiformes

Size Length: 18–20 in (46–51 cm); wingspan: 40–44 in (101–112 cm); weight: 1.5–2 lb (0.7–0.9 kg)

Key features Stout-bodied, with thick neck and short, diamond-shaped tail; flies on stiff wings; most have gray-and-white gull-like plumage, but many high Arctic breeders are darker overall; stubby, yellow bill with prominent tubular nostrils on top

Habits Gregarious at breeding sites; feeds at sea in scattered or dense flocks

Nesting Lays 1 white egg on bare rock ledge, a hollow, or a burrow; incubation 47–53 days by both sexes; young fledge after 46–53 days; 1 brood

Voice Range of loud cackling, chuckling, and crooning sounds at nest; soft cooing and sneezing calls in flight; feeding flocks grunt and cackle

Diet Fish, small squid, crustaceans, jellyfish, and other marine creatures; carrion from ships

Habitat Breeds mainly on cliffs, sometimes on ledges of buildings; otherwise lives on open oceans

Distribution Rocky coasts, islands, and open ocean throughout much of Arctic, northern Atlantic, and northern Pacific regions

Status Widespread, common, and increasing

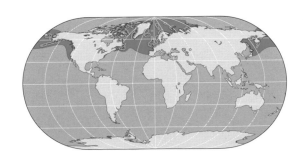

Brown Pelican

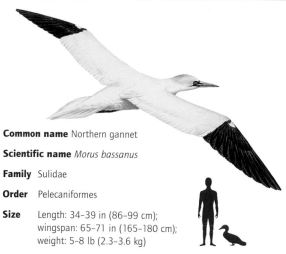

Common name Brown pelican

Scientific name *Pelecanus occidentalis*

Family Pelecanidae

Order Pelecaniformes

Size Length: 43–47 in (109–119 cm); wingspan: 75–85 in (190–216 cm); weight: 8–15 lb (3.6–6.8 kg)

Key features Typical huge pelican bill and throat pouch; mainly brown plumage; smaller and with less bright color on head and bill than similar Peruvian pelican

Habits Gregarious all year; plunges into sea from high in air to catch fish; young gather in crèches before fledging

Nesting Nests mainly in trees or shrubs; variable nest of sticks and grass; 2–3 chalky white eggs; incubation 28–31 days; young fledge after 63–78 days; 1 brood

Voice Adults make deep grunts, moans, and other sounds at breeding colonies; young utter higher-pitched noises, yelps, and screams

Diet Mainly fish; also carrion and crustaceans

Habitat Along coasts and islands, feeding in inshore waters, including estuaries; avoids open sea

Distribution Pacific coasts from British Columbia to Peru, including Galápagos; Atlantic coasts from New England through Caribbean to Guiana

Status Quite common; probably the second most numerous pelican after Peruvian pelican

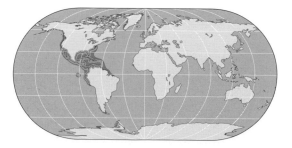

Northern Gannet

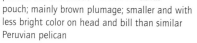

Common name Northern gannet

Scientific name *Morus bassanus*

Family Sulidae

Order Pelecaniformes

Size Length: 34–39 in (86–99 cm); wingspan: 65–71 in (165–180 cm); weight: 5–8 lb (2.3–3.6 kg)

Key features Very large white seabird; long, conical bill; long, streamlined body; long, pointed black-tipped wings; head and neck creamy-yellow; juveniles dark brown with white speckling, older immatures progressively more white

Habits Breeds mainly in large colonies; otherwise found in smaller groups that may gather at good feeding sites; plunges into sea for food

Nesting Nests on tops of steep cliffs, stacks, and islands; nests built of seaweed, grass, and flotsam; 1 pale blue egg; incubation 44 days by both sexes; young fledge after 90 days; 1 brood

Voice Chorus of loud, harsh groans, barks, and croaks at breeding colonies, with yapping sounds of young

Diet Shoaling open ocean fish, mainly mackerel, herring, sprat, and sand eels; also scavenges for offal and dead fish from fishing boats

Habitat Feeds at sea; breeds on mainland coasts and on offshore islands

Distribution Northern Atlantic, northern Caribbean, and western Mediterranean, from Arctic south to West Africa

Status Steady expansion of range and numbers; about 70 percent of total nest in British Isles

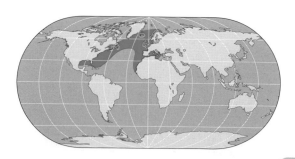

White-Tailed Tropicbird

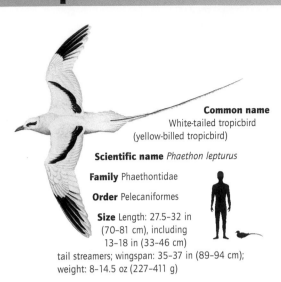

Common name
White-tailed tropicbird
(yellow-billed tropicbird)

Scientific name *Phaethon lepturus*

Family Phaethontidae

Order Pelecaniformes

Size Length: 27.5-32 in
(70-81 cm), including
13-18 in (33-46 cm)
tail streamers; wingspan: 35-37 in (89-94 cm);
weight: 8-14.5 oz (227-411 g)

Key features Graceful seabird with pointed wings and very long
central tail feathers; mainly white plumage, with black
markings through eye and on upper wings; Christmas
Island race has deep golden tinge to plumage

Habits Breeds in loose island colonies; wanders widely across
oceans when not breeding; catches fish by plunge-diving

Nesting Mainly on inaccessible cliff faces, in crevices, or
sheltered scrapes in soil, sometimes in tree hollows or
other sites; 1 egg; incubation 40-42 days; young fledge
after 70-85 days; 1 brood

Voice Loud whistles and harsh screams, especially
during courtship

Diet Small flying fish and squid; some crabs and
other invertebrates

Habitat Breeds on small, remote oceanic islands; spends most of
time roaming the open ocean; also seen along coasts

Distribution Almost all tropical and subtropical oceans apart
from eastern Pacific Ocean

Status Most numerous tropicbird, with major populations in
Caribbean and Indian Ocean, especially around
Christmas Island

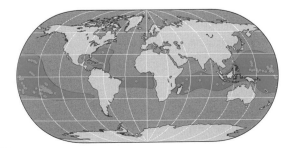

Herring Gull

Common name
Herring gull

Scientific name *Larus
argentatus*

Family Laridae

Order Charadriiformes

Size Length: 22-25 in (56-63.5 cm); wingspan: 53-57 in
(135-145 cm); weight: 1.5-3 lb (0.7-1.4 kg)

Key features Heavily built gull with large head and thick neck;
gray back and upper wings; wings have black tips with
white spots; rest of plumage white; strong yellow bill
with red spot at angle; head has dark streaks in winter

Habits Sociable, noisy, and bold; opportunist feeder at sea and
on land; usually breeds in colonies, vigorously defending
territory around nest

Nesting Nest of grass, seaweed, or other vegetation on open
ground, cliff ledge, or building; 2-3 brown-blotched, pale
green eggs; incubation 28-30 days; young fledge after
35-40 days; 1 brood

Voice Wide range of loud, mainly harsh calls

Diet Fish, crabs, worms, mollusks, insects, small mammals,
birds, eggs, fish offal, and garbage

Habitat Breeds mainly on or above sea cliffs, on dunes
or shingle beaches, and on roofs of coastal
buildings; outside breeding season more widespread,
including inland

Distribution North America, Europe, Scandinavia, and
northern Siberia, ranging south to Central America,
Japan, and China

Status Generally widespread and common; increase over
past century still continuing in many areas, but some
local decreases

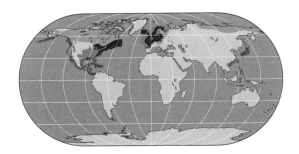

Arctic Tern

Common name Arctic tern

Scientific name *Sterna paradisaea*

Family Sternidae

Order Charadriiformes

Size Length: 13–14 in (33–36 cm); wingspan: 30–33 in (76–84 cm); weight: 3–4.5 oz (85–128 g)

Key features Mainly gray, with black cap (white at front in nonbreeding season); white cheeks, rump, and tail; narrow black line on trailing edge of wingtips; translucent "window" on hind wing; very long tail streamers; bill and very short legs blood-red, turning black in fall

Habits Feeds at sea by plunge-diving from hovering flight; breeds in small, widely dispersed colonies; exceptionally long migrations

Nesting Nest a shallow scrape; 2–3 eggs; incubation 22–27 days; young fledge after 21–24 days; 1 brood

Voice Very noisy, with loud, high-pitched rasping and clear piping or whistling calls

Diet Mainly small fish; also crustaceans, insects, krill, earthworms, and fish offal

Habitat Breeds mainly along coasts and inshore islands, but also far inland; generally migrates and winters well offshore

Distribution Mainly Arctic, but south to northern Europe, northwest and northeast U.S; winters in Southern Ocean

Status Widespread and common, but many populations have suffered serious declines

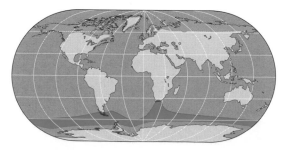

Great Skua

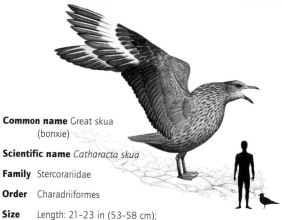

Common name Great skua (bonxie)

Scientific name *Catharacta skua*

Family Stercorariidae

Order Charadriiformes

Size Length: 21–23 in (53–58 cm); wingspan: 52–55 in (132–140 cm); weight: 2.5–3.8 lb (1.1–1.7 kg)

Key features Heavy body; broad-based wings; short tail; brown overall except for white, gold, ginger, and black flecks, and white "flashes" near wingtips; heavy, hooked bill; immature birds more uniformly brown with red tinge beneath

Habits Fiercely territorial at breeding grounds; usually seen alone outside breeding season, although gathers at rich feeding sites

Nesting Nests in loose colonies; usually 2 eggs; incubation 26–32 days mainly by female; young fledge after 40–51 days; 1 brood

Voice Soft, nasal alarm calls, and harsh screams or barks when attacking intruders

Diet Mainly sand eels and fish pirated from other birds, but also taken from sea surface; also seabirds, eggs, and young in breeding season

Habitat Breeds on damp, grassy moorland and other treeless habitats, often above sea cliffs; winters at sea, often far from land

Distribution Mainly northeastern Atlantic, north to Arctic; ranges south to Newfoundland, Brazil, and West Africa

Status Increasing in most parts of range; has recently colonized sites in the Arctic

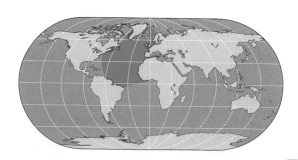

Black Skimmer

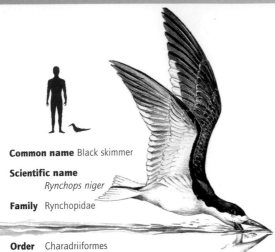

Common name Black skimmer

Scientific name *Rynchops niger*

Family Rynchopidae

Order Charadriiformes

Size Length: 16–18 in (41–46 cm); wingspan: 42–50 in (107–127 cm); weight: 8–10 oz (227–283 g)

Key features Large head; huge bill with elongated, knifelike lower mandible; slender body; very long, pointed wings and short tail; pied plumage contrasts with half-red, half-black bill and red feet

Habits Feeds in flight by "skimming" water surface, mainly at dusk and during night; breeds in small colonies and roosts in dense groups, often with terns and other seabirds

Nesting Nest a shallow depression in sand or shells; 3–4 eggs; incubation 21–26 days; young fledge after 28–30 days; 1 brood

Voice Barking calls, especially at breeding colonies

Diet Fish, plus shrimp and other crustaceans

Habitat Sheltered coastal waters; also large rivers and even high-altitude lakes in South America

Distribution Coastal U.S. to Central and South America, ranging south to southern Chile

Status Locally common in parts of its range, but very vulnerable to disturbance, habitat alteration, pollutants in fish prey, and predators

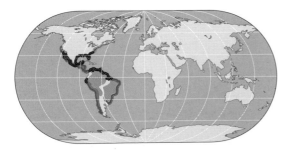

Atlantic Puffin

Common name Atlantic puffin

Scientific name *Fratercula arctica*

Family Alcidae

Order Charadriiformes

Size Length: 10–14 in (25.4–36 cm); wingspan: 18.5–25 in (47–63.5 cm); weight: 12–19 oz (340–539 g)

Key features Plump body; short wings with broad tips; neat black-and-white plumage; large white patch on head (grayish in winter); huge, triangular multicolored bill (duller in winter); bright orange legs (yellowish in winter)

Habits Feeds at sea by "flying" underwater to catch fish; breeds in colonies, often large and dense, defending nest area fiercely against rivals; usually solitary or in small, widely scattered groups in winter

Nesting Chamber, lined with grass and feathers, at end of a tunnel or in a crevice among rocks; 1 egg; incubation 36–45 days by both sexes; young fledge after 34–60 days; 1 brood

Voice Various growling calls at breeding colonies

Diet Mainly fish; adults also eat crustaceans and other marine invertebrates

Habitat Sea cliffs—on tops and terraces with low vegetation, in rock crevices, and among boulders; winters at sea

Distribution Coasts, islands, and open ocean throughout northern Atlantic, from Arctic to New England and Canary Islands

Status Despite many large breeding populations, numbers are fluctuating; threats include rats, foxes, and other predators at breeding colonies, overfishing, being caught in fishing nets, and oil pollution

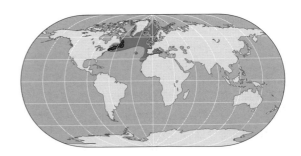

Black Guillemot

Common name Black guillemot

Scientific name *Cepphus grylle*

Family Alcidae

Order Charadriiformes

Size Length: 12–12.5 in (30–32 cm); wingspan: 20–23 in (51–58 cm); weight: 1–1.2 lb (0.45–0.5 kg)

Key features Breeding plumage wholly sooty-black with large white wing patches; retains white wing patches in nonbreeding (and juvenile) plumage, but has pale, dark-mottled upper parts and white underparts; bill black, but with bright red mouth; legs brilliant red

Habits Much less gregarious than typical auks; feeds underwater, making long dives to seabed

Nesting Nests among boulders on shore or in crevices usually low down in cliffs; usually 2 eggs; incubation 23–40 days; young fledge after 31–51 days; 1 brood

Voice Variety of shrill, high-pitched whistling and squeaking calls; sometimes trills during breeding season

Diet Mainly fish; also some marine invertebrates

Habitat Breeds along rocky and boulder-strewn shores; feeds only in shallow waters; winters near breeding areas except where ice prevents it in Arctic

Distribution Scattered around Arctic and north Atlantic coasts

Status Most populations fairly stable, but increases at some colonies and declines at others

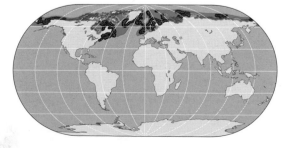

Ringed Plover

Common name Ringed plover (common ringed plover)

Scientific name *Charadrius hiaticula*

Family Charadriidae

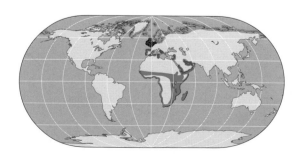

Order Charadriiformes

Size Length: 7–8 in (18–20 cm); wingspan: 19–22 in (48–56 cm); weight: 1.5–2.8 oz (42.5–79 g)

Key features Compact bird; black breast band and white collar; plumage mostly brown above with white wing bar, body white below; legs orange; sexes similar; juvenile has duller plumage with less distinct head pattern

Habits Darting runs along shore are punctuated with sudden stops to feed; often seen in flocks

Nesting Shallow scrape on sand or shingle; 3–4 eggs; incubation 23–25 days; young fledge after 24 days; 2 broods, sometimes 3

Voice Call a liquid, rising "too-lee"; also a piping "weep"; song is a melodious, rapid repetition of "teleea"

Diet Flies and small crustaceans on breeding grounds; mainly marine worms, crustaceans, and mollusks outside breeding season

Habitat Mainly coastal beaches, but also inland on edges of rivers and lakes; breeds inland on northern tundra

Distribution Virtually circumpolar in the north temperate and Arctic from Eurasia west through Iceland and Greenland to northeast Canada; also in coastal areas of central and southern Africa

Status Not globally threatened; decreasing in some parts of breeding due to human disturbance

Lapwing

Common name Lapwing (northern lapwing)

Scientific name *Vanellus vanellus*

Family Charadriidae

Order Charadriiformes

Size Length: 11–12 in (28–30.5 cm); wingspan: 32–34 in (81–86 cm); weight: 4.6–11.7 oz (130–332 g)

Key features Broad, round-tipped wings; long, slender crest at back of head; greenish-black above, mostly white below; sexes similar; juvenile has duller plumage and shorter crest

Habits Male performs a spectacular aerial display in breeding season; flocks form after breeding

Nesting Shallow scrape; usually 3–5 eggs; incubation 26–28 days; young fledge after 35–40 days; 1 brood, but new clutch laid if first lost

Voice A plaintive, piping "pee-wee"; in alarm a thin "u-wip"; territorial song a rich, bubbling sequence of calls, including "chee-o-wee"

Diet Wide variety of ground invertebrates such as beetles, flies, grasshoppers, and earthworms

Habitat Open country with bare ground or short grass, often farmland; also coasts and estuaries in winter

Distribution Throughout temperate Europe and Asia; wintering farther south to warmer latitudes, including North Africa; occasionally strays to North America

Status Not globally threatened, but declining in many intensively farmed regions

Spoon-Billed Sandpiper

Common name Spoon-billed sandpiper

Scientific name *Eurynorhynchus pygmeus*

Family Scolopacidae

Order Charadriiformes

Size Length: 6 in (15 cm); wingspan: 16 in (41 cm); weight: 1.1–1.2 oz (31–34 g)

Key features Tiny shorebird; unique spatulate bill tip; in breeding season upper parts striped black, buff, and rufous; face, neck, and breast chestnut-red streaked with brown, rest of underparts white; paler brownish-gray above in winter; juvenile similar

Habits Feeds with highly distinctive side-to-side sweeping movement of bill

Nesting Shallow mossy cup lined with leaves; 4 eggs; incubation 18–20 days; young fledge after 17–19 days; 1 brood

Voice Quiet "preep" or a shrill "wheet"; song a buzzing, descending "preer-prr-prr"

Diet Mainly insects; also small crustaceans and seeds

Habitat Breeds on coasts with thinly grassed, sandy ridges near freshwater pools and swampy ground; on coastal mudflats in winter

Distribution Coastal rim of northeast Siberia and on coasts from southeast India to Singapore and southeast China

Status Extremely rare; declining rapidly due to habitat loss, disturbance, and hunting

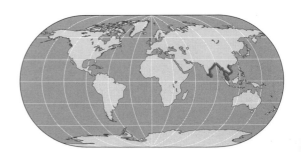

Snipe

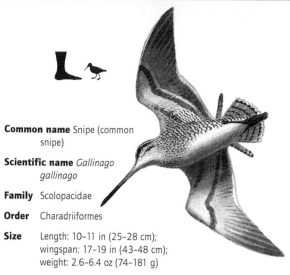

Common name Snipe (common snipe)

Scientific name *Gallinago gallinago*

Family Scolopacidae

Order Charadriiformes

Size Length: 10–11 in (25–28 cm); wingspan: 17–19 in (43–48 cm); weight: 2.6–6.4 oz (74–181 g)

Key features Medium-sized body; long, straight bill; dark brown plumage; striped head and back; sexes similar; juvenile has pale feather edges

Habits Zigzagging escape flight; makes characteristic drumming sound during display flight

Nesting Shallow, thinly lined scrape in dense grass or sedge; 4 eggs; incubation 18–20 days; young fledge after 19–20 days; 1 brood

Voice Hoarse "scaap" given when alarmed; male's song a monotonously repeated "chip-per"

Diet Mainly insects, worms, and mollusks; also some seeds

Habitat Mainly marshy ground, often with tussocky grass or sedges with soft, easily probed soil

Distribution Eurasia, Iceland, North America, Central and South America, Africa, Middle East, and Asia

Status Not globally threatened, but has decreased during the 20th century in regions subject to land improvement and drainage

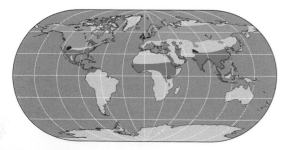

Knot

Common name Knot

Scientific name *Calidris canutus*

Family Scolopacidae

Order Charadriiformes

Size Length: 9–10 in (23–25 cm); wingspan: 22–24 in (56–61 cm); weight: 4.1–8.8 oz (116–249 g)

Key features Sturdy build; short bill; cinnamon body and grayish-white underwings in summer, mostly gray in winter; sexes similar; juvenile similar to nonbreeding adult

Habits Roosts in often massive, dense flocks that perform spectacular aerial maneuvers

Nesting Shallow, thinly lined scrape on open ground; 3–4 eggs; incubation 21–22 days; young fledge after 18–20 days; 1 brood

Voice A slightly hoarse "puk" outside breeding season; also a sharp, repeated "quee" in alarm; male's song a fluting "ko-u-ee"

Diet Mainly insects and plant material on breeding grounds; mainly small marine mollusks outside breeding season; also worms

Habitat Nests on Arctic tundra, mainly on raised ground near marsh or other water; winters on intertidal mudflats and beaches

Distribution Breeds in high Arctic Eurasia, Greenland, and Canada; winters on coast in southern U.S., South America, western Europe, west and southern Africa, East Indies, and Australasia

Status Not globally threatened; vulnerable to land reclamation and other coastal development

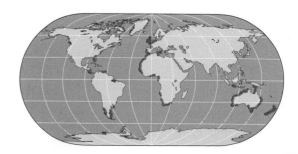

Pied Avocet

Common name Pied avocet

Scientific name *Recurvirostra avosetta*

Family Recurvirostridae

Order Charadriiformes

Size Length: 16.5-17.7 in (42-45 cm); wingspan: 30.3-31 in (77-79 cm); weight: 7.9-14 oz (224-397 g)

Key features Slender, upcurved bill; brilliant white plumage with thick black band running down back of head and neck; 3 black patches on wings that show as near-parallel stripes at rest; long, bluish-gray legs

Habits Wades through shallow water, swishing bill from side to side to catch food

Nesting Grass-lined scrape; usually 3-4 eggs; incubation 23-25 days; young fledge after 35-42 days; 1 brood

Voice Short "kluut" and similar calls

Diet Aquatic invertebrates, especially crustaceans; young chicks require insects

Habitat Lagoons, lakes, and estuaries

Distribution Europe, Central Asia, and southern Africa; also northern and Central Africa, Persian Gulf, northwest India, and southern China

Status Widespread and not globally threatened, although some threats to habitats in Asia

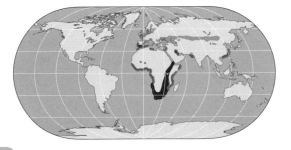

Eurasian Oystercatcher

Common name
Eurasian oystercatcher

Scientific name *Haematopus ostralegus*

Family Haematopodidae

Order Charadriiformes

Size Length: 15.7-19 in (40-48 cm); wingspan: 31.5-34 in (80-86 cm); weight: 15-29 oz (425-822 g)

Key features Bulky shorebird; short legs; long, thick orange-red bill; red eye ring; pied plumage with black head, chest, and back; white below; white half-collar in winter; sexes alike

Habits Ungainly walk; frequently probes ground with bill for food

Nesting Shallow scrape in variety of habitats, both coastal and inland; 2-4 eggs; incubation 24-35 days; young fledge after 33 days; 1 brood

Voice Variety of high, piping calls

Diet Mostly mollusks and crustaceans by coasts; earthworms and soil invertebrates inland

Habitat Mostly low-lying coasts; inland by rivers and in fields

Distribution Eastern Europe and northern coastal areas, northwestern Asia, Korea, and Kamchatka; also southern Europe, northwestern and eastern Africa, Arabian Gulf, India, and southeast China; isolated population in New Zealand

Status Widespread and common; European and New Zealand populations thought to be increasing, particularly inland

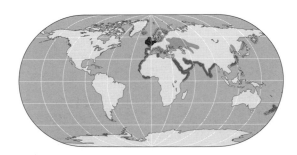

Common Loon

Common name
Common loon
(great northern diver)

Scientific name *Gavia immer*

Family Gaviidae

Order Gaviiformes

Size Length: 27–36 in (68.5–91 cm); wingspan: 50–57 in (127–147 cm); weight: 6.5–10 lb (3–4.5 kg); male slightly larger than female

Key features Heavily built, thick-necked bird; large head with big, pointed, blue-gray bill; sexes similar

Habits Almost totally aquatic; dives for food; pairs form lifelong bonds and nest well away from humans and other loons

Nesting Nest a heap of plant material close to water's edge; 1–3 eggs; incubation 24–25 days; young fledge after 63 days; 1 brood

Voice Yodeling and "tremelo" calls, and soft hoots

Diet Mainly fish, but also crustaceans, insects, mollusks, amphibians; also some vegetable matter

Habitat Large, deep freshwater lakes surrounded by conifer forests or tundra; flies south to winter on coasts and occasionally inland lakes—either alone, in pairs, or usually small flocks

Distribution Northern areas of the Northern Hemisphere and along coasts of North Atlantic and Pacific

Status Not globally threatened, but population has declined over the last 100 years, particularly as a result of human disturbance

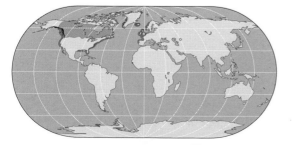

Great Crested Grebe

Common name Great crested grebe

Scientific name *Podiceps cristatus*

Family Podicipedidae

Order Podicipediformes

Size Length: 18–20 in (46–51 cm); wingspan: 33.5–35.5 in (85–90 cm); weight: 1.3–3.3 lb (0.6–1.5 kg)

Key features Long, narrow body, slender neck, angular head, tapering to long, thin beak; winter plumage dark above, light below; striking plumes in breeding season; sexes similar, but male has longer, heavier bill and, in the breeding season, a longer crest

Habits Highly visible; almost totally aquatic, nearly always on open water; dives for food

Nesting Early spring; mat of semisubmerged vegetation; usually 3–5 eggs; incubation 28 days; young fledge after 70–84 days; occasionally 2 broods

Voice Harsh, guttural calls made by both sexes

Diet Mainly fish, but also insects and crustaceans such as shrimp

Habitat Freshwater lakes and large ponds; may winter on estuaries or slow-moving rivers

Distribution Temperate areas of Europe and Asia; also highland lakes of southern Africa and Australasia

Status Not globally threatened; formerly hunted to near-extinction in many countries for its feathers; range and numbers have increased within last 100 years partly because of ability to make use of new manmade habitats such as reservoirs and other wetlands

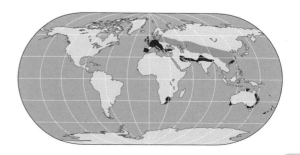

Gray Heron

American Bittern

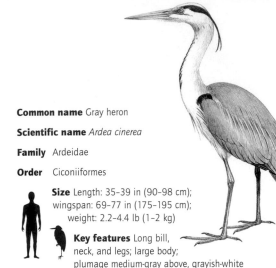

Common name Gray heron

Scientific name *Ardea cinerea*

Family Ardeidae

Order Ciconiiformes

Size Length: 35–39 in (90–98 cm); wingspan: 69–77 in (175–195 cm); weight: 2.2–4.4 lb (1–2 kg)

Key features Long bill, neck, and legs; large body; plumage medium-gray above, grayish-white below; sexes identical; juvenile has gray plumage and dull bare parts

Habits Stands motionless for long periods, often at water's edge, waiting for prey

Nesting Huge stick nest, often in colony; usually 3–5 eggs, exceptionally 1–10; incubation 25–26 days; young fledge after 50 days; occasionally 2 broods

Voice Loud "frank" call given in flight; squawks and yelps at nest

Diet Mainly fish, but also amphibians, crustaceans, water insects, mollusks, waterbirds, snakes, and mammals

Habitat All kinds of shallow water, including lakes, estuaries, marshes, and ricefields

Distribution Found in all but the most mountainous, dry, and cold parts of Europe, Africa, and Asia

Status Not globally threatened; heavily persecuted in past, particularly in Europe; now common and widespread

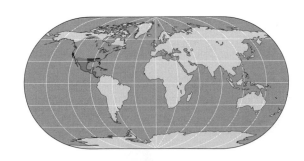

Common name American bittern

Scientific name *Botauris lentiginosus*

Family Ardeidae

Order Ciconiiformes

Size Length: 23.5–33.5 in (60–85 cm); wingspan: 41–49 in (105–125 cm); weight: 13–20 oz (0.4–0.6 kg)

Key features Thickset, medium-sized, streaky brown heron; small yellow bill; juvenile lacks the black line behind the eye broadening to a patch running down neck; sexes identical

Habits Solitary; normally secretive but occasionally seen stalking prey in open fields

Nesting Platform of vegetation in dense marsh cover; 3–5 eggs (exceptionally 2–7); incubation 28–29 days; young fledge after 14 days; 1 brood

Voice Male gives booming call in breeding season; alarm call is "kok-kok-kok"

Diet Very wide: fish, amphibians, snakes, small mammals, crawfish, mollusks, and insects

Habitat Marshes, bogs, open meadows; mangroves, and swamps outside breeding season

Distribution North and central U.S. states and southern Canada; also southern U.S., Central America, and Caribbean

Status Not globally threatened but declining throughout breeding range; declared as threatened or endangered in many U.S. states and Canadian provinces

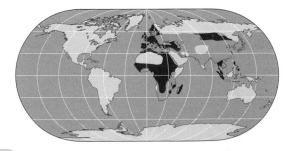

Wood Stork

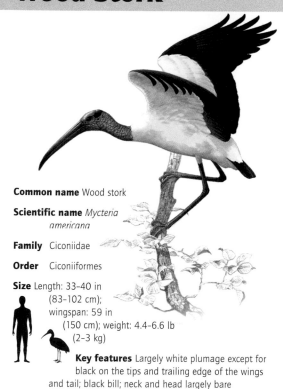

Common name Wood stork

Scientific name *Mycteria americana*

Family Ciconiidae

Order Ciconiiformes

Size Length: 33–40 in (83–102 cm); wingspan: 59 in (150 cm); weight: 4.4–6.6 lb (2–3 kg)

Key features Largely white plumage except for black on the tips and trailing edge of the wings and tail; black bill; neck and head largely bare

Habits Nests colonially; feeds in groups

Nesting In the tops of tall trees, often on islands; nest consists of a large pile of sticks lined with leaves; 3 eggs; incubation 28–32 days; young fledge after 65 days; 1 brood

Voice Normally silent but will hiss when at nest site during breeding season

Diet Mostly small fish; also invertebrates and small snakes

Habitat Shallow water in swamps, mangroves, estuaries, and manmade habitats such as canals; prefers fresh water

Distribution Wetland areas from northern Argentina, through Mexico, to North America

Status Not globally threatened but has suffered serious declines in the southeastern U.S.

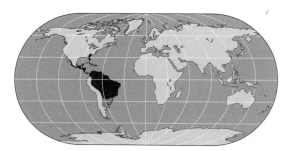

Greater Flamingo

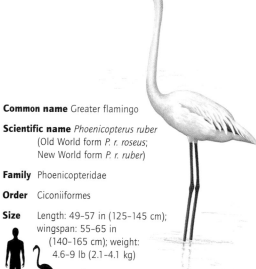

Common name Greater flamingo

Scientific name *Phoenicopterus ruber* (Old World form *P. r. roseus*; New World form *P. r. ruber*)

Family Phoenicopteridae

Order Ciconiiformes

Size Length: 49–57 in (125–145 cm); wingspan: 55–65 in (140–165 cm); weight: 4.6–9 lb (2.1–4.1 kg)

Key features (*P. r. roseus*): Overall pale pink with pink legs and a red-pink, downcurved bill tipped with black; wing-coverts crimson; flight feathers black. (*P. r. ruber*): Much redder plumage; bill orange-pink and black, with a yellowish base

Habits Highly social species rarely, if ever, seen alone

Nesting Nest a low mound of mud or sand; 1 egg (rarely 2); incubation 28–31 days; young fledge after about 75 days; 1 brood

Voice Loud, gooselike honking call

Diet Feeds by filtering small invertebrates and plant matter from mud; food includes insects, mollusks, and crustaceans

Habitat Shallow lagoons, saltpans, and tidal mudflats

Distribution In Old World in parts of southern Europe, Africa, Middle East, and India; in New World in Galápagos, Central America, Caribbean islands, and northern South America

Status Not globally threatened

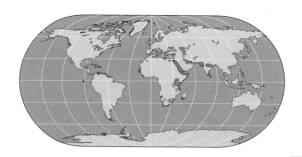

Mute Swan

Common name Mute swan

Scientific name *Cygnus olor*

Family Anatidae

Order Anseriformes

Size Length: 49–63 in (125–160 cm); wingspan: 94 in (240 cm); weight: 14–33 lb (6.6–15 kg)

Key features Large, long-necked bird; adults white, juveniles brownish; females normally smaller than males with smaller knob on bill

Habits Usually on or near water; may be in pairs or family groups; often in close proximity to man—some individuals very approachable

Nesting Spring and summer; nest is a large pile of vegetation, sometimes floating; 5–7 eggs; incubation 35–36 days; young fledge at 120–150 days; 1 brood

Voice Not mute! Threatened birds hiss; other sounds include snoring, snorting, quiet trumpeting, and bubbling noises; whooshing noise heard in flight is caused by wings

Diet Mostly aquatic plants; also seeds, grasses, and herbs taken at the water's edge or when grazing on land; occasionally small animals

Habitat Lowland freshwater lakes (including manmade bodies of water), marshes, rivers, and estuaries; also sheltered sea areas

Distribution Resident populations in northern and central Europe and North America; migrant populations in eastern Europe, Scandinavia, Central Asia, and eastern China; small, feral, nonmigrating populations in South Africa, Australia, New Zealand, and Japan

Status Not threatened; range expanding due to originally ornamental swans establishing feral populations

Canada Goose

Common name Canada goose

Scientific name *Branta canadensis*

Family Anatidae

Order Anseriformes

Size Length: 22–43 in (55–110 cm); wingspan: 48–72 in (122–183 cm); weight: 4.5–14 lb (2–6.4 kg); male larger

Key features Black neck and head; white cheek patches joining under chin; body mostly brown, with white on lower belly extending to undertail

Habits Common; found in a range of habitats, usually near water; may form large flocks

Nesting Nest built on ground from plant material, lined with feathers; 4–7 eggs; incubation 24–30 days; young fledge after 40–86 days; 1 brood

Voice Large subspecies make a deep honk; smaller subspecies make a higher-pitched cackle or barking noise

Diet Seeds, fruit, and grain on land; also underwater plant material such as roots and stems

Habitat Tundra, semidesert, open cultivated areas, and wooded areas, usually near water

Distribution Native to North America; introduced to Britain, northwest Europe, and New Zealand

Status Common and not globally threatened, although some subspecies are declining; Aleutian islands subspecies (*B. c. leucopareia*) has benefited from conservation action

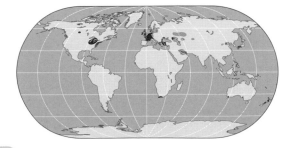

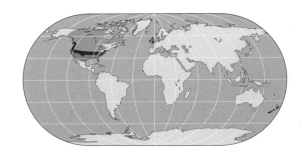

Mallard

Common name Mallard

Scientific name *Anas platyrhynchos*

Family Anatidae

Order Anseriformes

Size Length: 20-26in (50-65cm); wingspan: 29-39in (75-100cm); weight: 1.6-3.4 lb (0.7-1.5 kg)

Key features Male grayish with brown chest, thin white ring around neck, bottle-green upper neck and head, and black-and-white stern; female mostly brown with darker streaks; both sexes have blue speculum

Habits Common on water, often in groups or with other waterbirds; dabbles and upends in water for food

Nesting Spring and summer; nest is built of grass lined with feathers and normally on the ground; 9-13 eggs; incubation 27-28 days; young fledge after 50-60 days; 1 brood

Voice Female makes familiar quacking noise; male's voice weaker and more rasping

Diet An opportunist; plant material includes seeds and leaves; animals include insects, mollusks, worms, and rarely fish and amphibians

Habitat Within its range found in almost all types of water—freshwater, brackish, and seawater; avoids fast-flowing streams and rivers and nutrient-poor waters

Distribution Throughout temperate latitudes in Northern Hemisphere; introduced to southeast Australia and New Zealand

Status Probably the commonest duck; in 1991 around 18 million wintered in North America despite being a common quarry for hunters

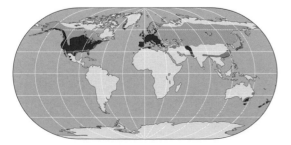

Mandarin Duck

Common name Mandarin duck

Scientific name *Aix galericulata*

Family Anatidae

Order Anseriformes

Size Length: 16-20 in (41-50 cm); wingspan: 27-29 in (68-74 cm); weight: 15.5-17.5 oz (0.4-0.5 kg)

Key features Small, long-tailed duck; male multicolored with crest, ruff, and prominent wing "sails"; female and juvenile duller with predominate gray, brown, and green plumage coloration

Habits Shy, intolerant of human disturbance; waterside feeder both by day and night

Nesting Nests in tree holes and stumps; 9-12 eggs; incubation 28-30 days; young fledge after about 42 days; 1 brood

Voice Short courtship and alarm calls given by both sexes

Diet Seeds, nuts, and aquatic plants; also insects, mollusks, and fish

Habitat Rivers, lakes, pools, and swamps surrounded by dense forest

Distribution Found in Japan, China, Korea, and Siberia; feral population in Britain

Status Not threatened, but declining in China and Korea as a result of deforestation

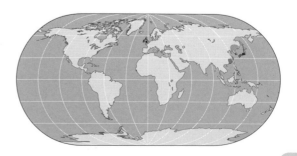

King Eider

Common name King eider

Scientific name *Somateria spectabilis*

Family Anatidae

Order Anseriformes

Size Length: 18.5-25 in (47-63.5 cm); wingspan: 34-40 in (86-101 cm); weight: 3-4.5 lb (1.4-2 kg)

Key features Breeding male mainly black body with small "sails" on back, salmon-pink breast, black wings with white forewing patches, bulbous multicolored head; dark in eclipse plumage; female has shorter, darker bill than common eider, with dark "smiling" gape and warmer, reddish-brown plumage with more crescent-shaped black bars; juveniles resemble female

Habits Feeds mainly in coastal waters, taking prey from seabed; highly gregarious outside breeding season, but typically nesting in pairs

Nesting Nest usually near water; a hollow lined mainly with down from female's breast; 3-7 pale olive eggs; incubation by female for 22-24 days; fledging period unknown; 1 brood

Voice Male utters deep, vibrating cooing calls during courtship displays; main calls of female deep, hoarse clucking sounds

Diet Mollusks, crustaceans, and echinoderms; also eelgrass and aquatic insects

Habitat Breeds mainly inland on Arctic tundra, by freshwater pools, sometimes by rivers and along seacoasts; winters along seacoasts

Distribution Throughout Arctic, ranging south to northwestern Atlantic and north Pacific

Status Populations generally stable, but locally birds are threatened by oil pollution

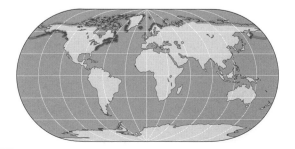

Whooping Crane

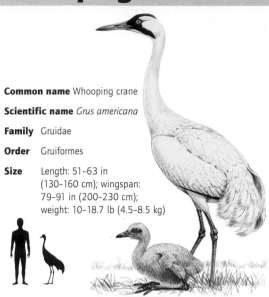

Common name Whooping crane

Scientific name *Grus americana*

Family Gruidae

Order Gruiformes

Size Length: 51-63 in (130-160 cm); wingspan: 79-91 in (200-230 cm); weight: 10-18.7 lb (4.5-8.5 kg)

Key features Large, mainly white crane; dark legs, black primary feathers; gray beak and red crown

Habits Territorial during the breeding season; social outside the breeding season

Nesting Nest a mound of vegetation up to 59 in (150 cm) diameter and 18 in (46 cm) above the surface of the water; 2 eggs; incubation 28-31 days; young fledge after 90 days: 1 brood

Voice Loud trumpeting calls

Diet Small aquatic invertebrates, frogs, snakes, and fish; also plant matter such as grain

Habitat Breeds on "muskeg" and marshy pools; found on prairies during migration; winters on coastal marshes

Distribution Only wild population breeds in Wood Buffalo National Park, Canada, and winters at Aransas on the Texas coast

Status Endangered; 161 adults and 15 chicks at Aransas National Wildlife Refuge in 2001, but numbers increasing gradually, reaching a total of 213 in 2004

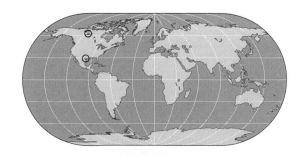

Common Moorhen

Common name Common moorhen

Scientific name *Gallinula chloropus*

Family Rallidae

Order Gruiformes

Size Length: 12–15 in (30–38 cm); wingspan: 19.5–21.5 in (50–55 cm); weight: 7–17 oz (0.2–0.5 kg)

Key features Generally dark plumage except for white streaking on the flanks and white tail panels; beak red, tipped with yellow; legs olive-yellow with long, unwebbed toes

Habits Territorial and rarely forms flocks; common but shy—quickly slips away from disturbance

Nesting Nest built in newly emerging vegetation or on solid ground within a wetland in spring and summer; occasionally they make floating nests and will also nest low in bushes, but never more than a few feet from water; usually 6–8 eggs; incubation 21–22 days; young fledge after 50 days; 2 broods, occasionally 3 or 4

Voice A distinctive "kruuuk"

Diet A wide range of animal and plant matter, including small invertebrates and carrion

Habitat Wide range of mainly freshwater habitats

Distribution With 12 separate subspecies stretching across all but one of the world's continents, the common moorhen is the most widely distributed gallinule; the only places it is not found are Australia and New Zealand, where it is replaced by dusky moorhen (*G. tenebrosa*)

Status Not globally threatened overall, but two island subspecies are listed as Endangered

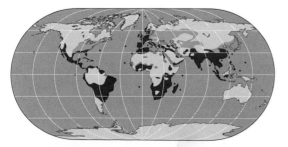

Great Bustard

Common name Great bustard

Scientific name *Otis tarda*

Family Otididae

Order Gruiformes

Size Length: 29.5–41 in (75–104 cm); wingspan: 75–102 in (190–260 cm); weight: up to 53 lb (24 kg)

Key features Massive bustard with boldly barred, tawny-brown upper side; mainly white underside and wings; male has gray head and orange-chestnut breastband

Habits Lives in small groups or flocks in open spaces; mostly terrestrial but flying powerfully at times

Nesting Nest is a scrape on the ground sparsely lined with grass; 2–3 eggs; incubation 21–28 days; young fledge after 30–35 days; 1 brood

Voice Short, barking croaks, but mostly silent

Diet Shoots, leaves, buds, seeds; also insects, small reptiles, and a few small young birds

Habitat Open grassland, semiarid steppe and river valleys

Distribution Widespread but extremely localized; Iberia eastward across mid-Europe into Central Asia and some parts of eastern Asia

Status Rare and declining in most of its range; seriously threatened in much of its European distribution

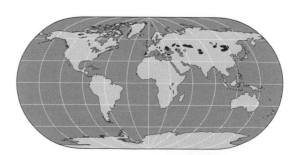

Osprey

Common name Osprey

Scientific name *Pandion haliaetus*

Family Pandionidae

Order Falconiformes

Size Length: 22–23 in (56–58.5 cm); wingspan: 57–67 in (145–170 cm); weight: 2.6–4.3 lb (1.2–2 kg); female slightly larger than male

Key features Long, narrow wings; dark-brown upper parts and mainly white underparts with dark-speckled breast band; white head with dark-brown stripe through yellow eye; black hooked bill; blue-gray legs; sexes identical; immature paler

Habits Hunts alone over shallow water; spends much time perched near water

Nesting Large, isolated nest of sticks and grasses, usually in top of tall tree near water; season varies with region; usually 2–3 eggs; incubation 35–43 days; young fledge after 44–59 days; 1 brood

Voice Loud yelping call; shrill "pyew-pyew-pyew" during territorial display

Diet Mainly live fish snatched from just below surface of water, plus a few frogs, snakes, and small birds

Habitat Coasts, estuaries, rivers, lakes, and swamps

Distribution Breeds virtually worldwide except South America, polar regions, deserts, and much of Africa; breeding birds from North America and northern Eurasia winter in warm-temperate and tropical zones

Status Badly affected by pesticide poisoning during 1960s and 1970s, but now flourishing throughout most of its range

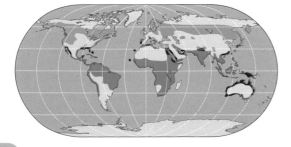

Peregrine Falcon

Common name Peregrine falcon

Scientific name *Falco peregrinus*

Family Falconidae

Order Falconiformes

Size Length: 14–20 in (35.5–51 cm); wingspan: 35–47 in (89–119 cm); weight: 1.3–3.3 lb (0.6–1.5 kg); female bigger and heavier than male

Key features Stocky; long, pointed wings; blue-gray upper parts; white to buff-pink underparts with dark bars; gray-black head with dark "mustache" and white chin; dark bill with yellow base; dark eye with yellow eye ring; yellow legs with black talons; sexes identical except for size; juvenile browner

Habits Aerial hunter; sights prey from perch or in patrolling flight; usually solitary

Nesting Nests on remote cliff ledge—sometimes on a building—with no nesting material; usually 3–4 eggs; incubation 28–32 days; young fledge after 35–42 days; 1 brood

Voice Raucous, high-pitched "kek-kek-kek-kek" alarm call; creaking "wee-chew"

Diet Mainly medium-sized birds such as pigeons, caught in flight, plus small mammals and insects

Habitat Very variable, from remote mountain wildernesses to city centers, but typically sea cliffs and crags; avoids extensive, dense forest

Distribution Virtually worldwide except Central Asia, central Sahara, Amazonia, Antarctica, and central Greenland; northern birds migrate south in winter

Status Has now recovered from serious declines in 1950s to 1970s caused by pesticide poisoning; still threatened in places

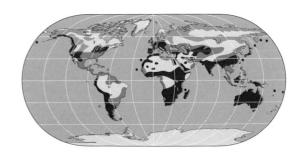

Everglade Kite

Common name Everglade kite
(snail kite)

Scientific name *Rostrhamus sociabilis* (Florida race:
R. s. plumbeus)

Family Accipitridae

Order Falconiformes

Size Length: 16–18 in (41–46 cm); wingspan: 45 in (114 cm);
weight: 13–14 oz (369–397 g)

Key features Slim and broad-winged; very slender, long-hooked
bill and red eye; male slate-gray with black wingtips and
white on tail, bare red skin on face, and red legs; female
brown with paler streaked underparts, orange skin on
face and legs; immature resembles female, but has
brown eye

Habits Very sociable, roosting and feeding together

Nesting Nests in loose colonies; builds stick nests in reed beds,
bushes, or trees; season varies with latitude; usually 2–4
eggs; incubation 26–28 days; young fledge after 40–49
days, but may leave nest earlier; 1–3 broods

Voice Bleating cry during courtship display

Diet Normally freshwater apple snails of the genus *Pomacea*;
also crabs and mice when snails are scarce

Habitat Marshes

Distribution Florida Everglades, Cuba, southeast Central
America, South America east of Andes

Status Rare, local, and vulnerable in Florida; common and
widespread elsewhere

Bald Eagle

Common name Bald eagle

Scientific name *Haliaeetus
leucocephalus*

Family Accipitridae

Order Falconiformes

Size Length: 28–38 in (71–96.5 cm); wingspan: 66–96 in
(168–244 cm); weight: 6.6–13.9 lb (3–6.3 kg);
female larger than male; northern race,
H. l. washingtoniensis, larger than southern race,
H. l. leucocephalus

Key features Large eagle with powerful yellow bill; yellow eyes
and legs; white head and tail; dark-brown body and
wings; sexes identical except for size; juvenile mottled
white with dark bill and eye

Habits Normally seen singly or in pairs, but gathers in larger
numbers to exploit rich food sources

Nesting Large stick nest, usually in a conifer tree or on a cliff
30–60 ft (9–18 m) above the ground; reused and added
to each year; nests in summer in north, winter in south;
usually 2 eggs; incubation 34–36 days; young fledge
after 70–92 days; 1 brood

Voice A squeaky cackle

Diet Mainly fish; also ducks, rabbits, rodents, turtles, snakes,
and carrion

Habitat Usually near open water in all kinds of terrain ranging
from cold conifer forest to hot deserts

Distribution Most of North America from southern Alaska and
Canada to northern Mexico, plus Aleutian Islands

Status Hit by persecution and pesticide poisoning in the past
but now flourishing, especially in far northwest of range

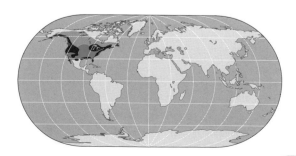

Northern Goshawk

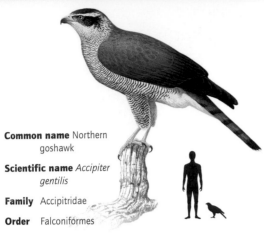

Common name Northern goshawk

Scientific name *Accipiter gentilis*

Family Accipitridae

Order Falconiformes

Size Length: 19–27 in (48–68.5 cm); wingspan: 38–50 in (96.5–127 cm); weight: 1.1–3.3 lb (0.5–1.5 kg); female much bigger and heavier than male

Key features Big, short-winged forest hawk with medium-long tail; yellow bill base and legs; orange-yellow eye; brown-gray above, pale below with dark bars; very variable over large range; female browner above; juvenile resembles female

Habits Lone woodland hunter, using ambush and pursuit from perch

Nesting Forms longstanding pairs in spring, often reoccupying old nest; usually 3–4 eggs, rarely 5; incubation 35–41 days; young fledge after 35–40 days; 1 brood

Voice Harsh "gek-gek-gek" alarm call, plus mewing "pee-yah" from female

Diet Mainly birds ranging from medium-sized songbirds to grouse and pheasants, plus small mammals

Habitat Typically coniferous or mixed woodlands and forests with clearings

Distribution Forests of northern North America, Europe, Scandinavia, Russia, Siberia, and Japan; in winter North American birds may migrate south as far as northern Mexico

Status Recovering from sharp decline caused by persecution, forest destruction, and pesticide poisoning during 19th to late 20th centuries

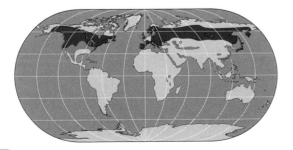

Golden Eagle

Common name Golden eagle

Scientific name *Aquila chrysaetos*

Family Accipitridae

Order Falconiformes

Size Length: 30–35 in (76–89 cm); wingspan: 75–89 in (190–226 cm); weight: 6.4–14.8 lb (2.9–6.7 kg); female bigger and heavier than male

Key features Very large with long, broad wings; mainly dark brown with golden-brown crown, nape, and wing coverts; brown eye; black-tipped bill; heavily feathered legs, yellow feet; sexes identical except for size; juvenile darker, with white patches on wings and tail

Habits Hunts on the wing, soaring and gliding, alone or in pairs

Nesting Builds big stick nest on crag or in tree in spring; usually 2 eggs, rarely 1–3; incubation 41–45 days; young fledge after 63–80 days, typically only 1 chick survives; 1 brood

Voice Generally silent, but gives whistling "twee-oo" of alarm and shrill "kya" at nest

Diet Mainly small mammals and game birds, plus carrion, but very variable

Habitat Wild, open terrain—often mountainous—from sea level to summer snow line

Distribution North America, wilder parts of Europe, Scandinavia, northern and Central Asia, North Africa; absent from most of Arctic

Status Recovering from heavy persecution, but still threatened by loss of habitat and food supply

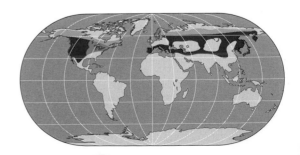

Lammergeier

Common name Lammergeier (bearded vulture)

Scientific name *Gypaetus barbatus*

Family Accipitridae

Order Falconiformes

Size Length: 39–45 in (99–114 cm); wingspan: 98–113 in (249–287 cm); weight: 10–16 lb (4.5–7.3 kg)

Key features Very large with long, pointed wings; long, wedge-shaped tail; face feathered with black beardlike tuft of feathers hanging over bill; head, neck, and underparts warm rust color; wings, tail, and back slaty-gray; juveniles dark brown, paler on mantle and underparts

Habits Patrols mountainsides with scarcely a wingbeat; wings held slightly arched down when gliding; lives solitarily or in pairs

Nesting Nest of sticks in cave; 2 eggs, but only 1 survives; incubation 53–58 days; young fledge after 106–130 days; 1 brood

Voice Usually silent, but makes screaming or whistling calls when displaying

Diet Carrion, especially bones; also live tortoises

Habitat Mountain ranges

Distribution Southern Europe, northwest, East, and South Africa, western Arabian Peninsula, Central Asia, and Himalayas

Status Near threatened; declining in Europe, western Asia, and in both North and South Africa

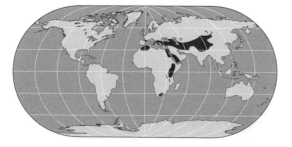

Turkey Vulture

Common name Turkey vulture

Scientific name *Cathartes aura*

Family Cathartidae

Order Falconiformes

Size Length: 25–32 in (64–81 cm); wingspan: 67–79 in (170–201 cm); weight: 1.9–4.4 lb (0.9–2 kg)

Key features Relatively long, broad wings; mainly black with brownish back, two-toned in flight with paler flight feathers and tail; small, naked red head; juveniles browner than adults

Habits Spends much time soaring, holding its wings in a shallow V; flies forward with slow wingbeats; unstable appearance in the air

Nesting Lays eggs on ground in cave or tree hole, sometimes under vegetation; 2 eggs; incubation 38–41 days; young fledge after 70–80 days; 1 brood

Voice Not very vocal; utters odd hiss or cluck

Diet Carrion

Habitat Broad range from deserts to rain forest

Distribution Throughout North and South America as far north as southern Canada

Status Not threatened

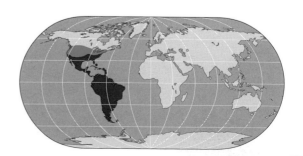

California Condor

Common name California condor

Scientific name *Gymnogyps californianus*

Family Cathartidae

Order Falconiformes

Size Length: 46–52 in (117–132 cm); wingspan: 109 in (277 cm); weight: 23 lb (10.4 kg)

Key features Very long, broad wings with prominent "fingers" at tips; plumage largely black, white triangle on underside of wings; head and neck pink, with small black ruff; juveniles have dark head and neck

Habits Soars on level (or slightly raised) wings, searching for prey; very stable in the air

Nesting No nest; lays egg on ground in cave or large tree hole; 1 egg; incubation 55–60 days; young fledge after 180 days; 1 brood

Voice Hissing and grunting at nest; otherwise silent

Diet Carrion, mainly from large carcasses

Habitat Hills and plains

Distribution California and Arizona: population extinct in the wild in 1987, but now reintroduced into these two states

Status Critically Endangered

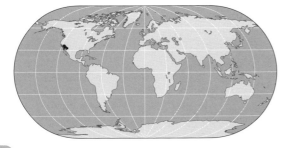

Secretary Bird

Common name Secretary bird

Scientific name *Sagittarius serpentarius*

Family Sagittariidae

Order Falconiformes

Size Length: 49–59 in (125–150 cm); wingspan: 83 in (211 cm); weight: 5–9.4 lb (2.3–4.3 kg)

Key features Very large, with a unique shape: long, almost cranelike legs, half feathered in black, plus long, pointed wings and long, graduated tail; bare, red face; typical raptor's bill; long, wispy crest, largely ash-gray plumage, but black crest, wings, tail tip, belly, and leg tops

Habits Terrestrial, usually seen walking on ground with measured steps; roosts in tree; sometimes flies, even soars; usually in pairs

Nesting Any time of year; large nest a platform of sticks in a thorn-tree canopy and lined with grass; usually 2 eggs; incubation 42–46 days; young fledge after 65–106 days; sometimes several broods in succession under good conditions

Voice Silent except at nest, where it makes a hoarse growling, deeper than most birds of prey

Diet Mainly insects, especially grasshoppers and beetles; also small vertebrates such as snakes, small mammals, and birds

Habitat Steppe and savanna, with short grass and thorn trees

Distribution Sub-Saharan Africa, except west-central Africa and the Horn of Africa

Status Not threatened

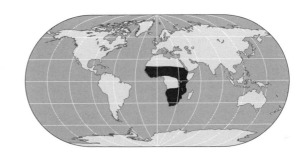

Snowy Owl

Common name Snowy owl

Scientific name *Nyctea scandiaca*

Family Strigidae

Order Strigiformes

Size Length: 21–26 in (53.5–66 cm); wingspan: 56–65 in (142–165 cm); weight: 1.6–6.5 lb (0.7–2.9 kg); female bigger than male

Key features Large and thickset, with massive, heavily feathered feet; golden-yellow eyes; male white with dark spots and bars; female has dark-brown bars; juvenile gray-brown with white face and brown-barred wings and tail

Habits Nomadic; typically hunts from perch at dusk and dawn, but active all hours in daylight of Arctic summer; winter activity uncertain

Nesting Nests in shallow scrape on ground, usually on hummock, in northern summer; usually 3–9 eggs, rarely up to 14; incubation 31–33 days; young fledge after 43–50 days; 1 brood

Voice Male has loud, booming territorial hoot; female has hooting, whistling, or mewing notes; alarm call a repeated, cackling "kre-kre-kre-kre"

Diet Lemmings, voles; also rabbits, hares, game birds, wildfowl, occasional fish, and insects

Habitat Mainly open, low tundra; also mountains and moorland, meadows, and salt marsh

Distribution Found throughout the Arctic tundra zones of North America, Scandinavia, and Asia; often moves south in winter or if prey populations crash

Status Scarce but widespread throughout range; numbers probably slightly reduced by some loss of wild habitat

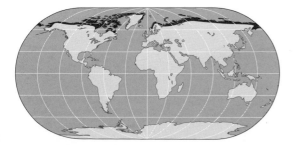

Barn Owl

Common name Barn owl

Scientific name *Tyto alba*

Family Tytonidae

Order Strigiformes

Size Length: 12–17 in (30.5–43 cm); wingspan: 33–37 in (84–95 cm); weight: 7–25 oz (198–709 g); female larger than male

Key features Medium-sized owl; heart-shaped face; dark eyes; long, densely feathered legs; plumage very variable, typically golden-buff and gray with dark spots above, dark-spotted white to buff below; many races darker above, with orange-buff underparts; juveniles similar

Habits Normally hunts alone at night, patrolling open ground with low, slow buoyant flight; also hunts from perch; occasionally active by day

Nesting Typically uses hole in tree or cliff, ruin, or farm building, sometimes abandoned bird nest; usually 4–7 eggs, but up to 16; incubation 29–34 days, young fledge after 55–65 days; 1–2 broods, rarely 3

Voice Shrill, eerie shriek; also snoring, wheezing, hissing, and yapping sounds at nest

Diet Small mammals such as mice and voles; also small birds, reptiles, frogs, fish, and insects

Habitat Favors farmland, grassland, or marshes; needs hollow trees, rock crevices, barns, or ruined buildings for nesting

Distribution America south of Great Lakes, western Europe, Africa except Sahara Desert, southwest and southern Asia, Southeast Asia, and Australia

Status Not globally threatened; declining in North America and Europe through pesticide use and loss of grassland habitat and nest sites

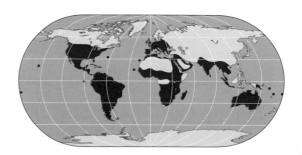

Budgerigar

Common name Budgerigar

Scientific name
Melopsittacus
undulatus

Family Psittacidae

Order Psittaciformes

Size Length: 7 in (18 cm);
wingspan: 10 in (25 cm); weight: 1 oz (28 g)

Key features Small, slender, sparrow-sized parrot with long
wings and tail; small, hooked bill; mostly apple-green
with bluish tail, yellow on head; wings and head
patterned with scales; domestic birds include blue
and yellow varieties; sexes similar, but male has blue
skin above the bill (blue-gray in breeding season),
while female has brown skin (brownish-pink in
breeding season)

Habits Roams in nomadic, noisy cohesive flocks, usually of
about 100 birds

Nesting Builds nest in tree hollow, often in loose colony; 4–6
white eggs, occasionally up to 8; incubation 18–20 days,
by female only; young fledge after 35 days; often
several clutches laid in quick succession

Voice Chirruping call

Diet Seeds and grain

Habitat A wide variety of open habitats, including savanna
and farmland

Distribution Inland Australia

Status Abundant

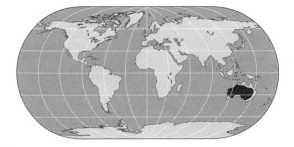

Scarlet Macaw

Common name Scarlet macaw

Scientific name Ara macao

Family Psittacidae

Order Psittaciformes

Size Length: 33–35 in (84–89 cm);
wingspan: 55 in (140 cm); weight: 2–3 lb
(0.9–1.5 kg)

Key features Very large parrot with outsize bill, long
wings, and very long tail; mainly scarlet with blue-
and-yellow wings; light-blue rump and undertail;
upper mandible pale yellow, lower mandible black;
bare cheek with white skin; gray feet; juveniles have
shorter tail

Habits Flies with slow, measured wingbeats, often quite high
over forest; often in small groups

Nesting No nest; uses large tree hole, often high above ground;
1–4 eggs; incubation 24–28 days; young fledge after
14 weeks; 1 brood

Voice Very loud croaking screech; also makes squawks and
growling sounds

Diet Wide variety of plant parts, including seeds, flowers,
leaves, fruit, and even bark

Habitat Lowland forest and savanna, often near rivers

Distribution Local in Central America, from eastern Honduras
and Nicaragua to Colombia; much commoner and more
widespread in lowland Amazonia

Status Central American race threatened by habitat destruction
and trapping for cage-bird trade; South American race
still common

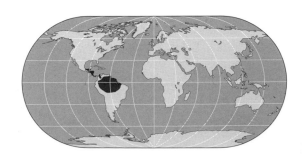

Kea

Common name Kea

Scientific name *Nestor notabilis*

Family Psittacidae

Order Psittaciformes

Size Length: 19 in (48 cm); wingspan: 40–42 in (101–107 cm); weight: 2 lb (0.9 kg)

Key features Large, plump parrot; long, curved upper mandible, shorter in female; scaly plumage, mostly brown on head, neck, and underparts, but iridescent bronze-green on wings and tail and bright orange patch under the wings; bluish tinge to primaries; chestnut rump

Habits Feeds mainly on the ground; often tame; juveniles form flocks in fall

Nesting Nest in crevice under rock or in hollow log, built from lichens, twigs, and leaves; 2–4 eggs; incubation 3–4 weeks; young fledge after 91 days; 1 brood

Voice A noisy "keea"

Diet Flowers, berries, leaves, and fruits, plus carrion and garbage; rarely small mammals

Habitat Mountain scrub, adjacent forests and valleys, mainly at 2,000–6,500 ft (600–1,980 m)

Distribution South Island of New Zealand

Status Near threatened because of restricted range

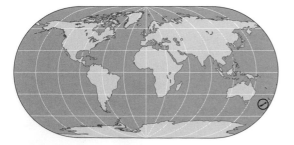

Cockatiel

Common name Cockatiel

Scientific name *Nymphicus hollandicus*

Family Cacatuidae

Order Psittaciformes

Size Length: 13 in (33 cm); wingspan: 18 in (46 cm); weight: 3–3.5 oz (85–100 g)

Key features Typical parrot shape, with large head and hooked bill; slim, with long wings and tail; perky upward-pointing crest; mainly gray, with large white wing and shoulder patches; lemon-yellow on face, with tomato-colored cheek spot; face colors more intense on male

Habits Sociable, living in flocks; nomadic, often flying long distances; fast flight

Nesting In tree hollow near water; makes "nest" platform of wood dust; usually 5 white eggs (2–8 known); incubation 18–20 days by both sexes; young fledge after 28–35 days; 1–3 broods

Voice Far-carrying, whistling "weero-weero"

Diet Small seeds, gathered from ground

Habitat Arid and semiarid open country

Distribution Inland Australia

Status Abundant

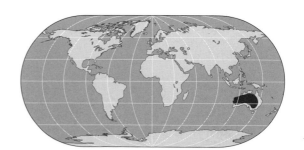

Pileated Woodpecker

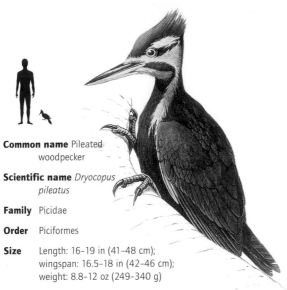

Common name Pileated woodpecker

Scientific name *Dryocopus pileatus*

Family Picidae

Order Piciformes

Size Length: 16–19 in (41–48 cm); wingspan: 16.5–18 in (42–46 cm); weight: 8.8–12 oz (249–340 g)

Key features Big, long-billed woodpecker; black plumage with white streaks along head and neck; red crown with crest; female has black forehead, male has red forehead and red "mustache" stripe; juvenile browner, with paler crown

Habits Largely solitary; feeds both in trees and on ground; not particularly shy around people

Nesting Excavates hole in large tree at a height of 20–40 ft (6–12 m); 2–4 eggs; incubation 18 days; young fledge after 26–28 days; 1 brood

Voice Loud "wuk" or "cac," either singly or repeated; drums with two-second rolls once or twice a minute

Diet Invertebrates, especially ants; also nuts, fruits, and berries

Habitat Old-growth forests and woodlands with large, old trees; also some secondary woodlands and town parks with older trees

Distribution From British Columbia across southern Canada and through eastern U.S. to Florida

Status Increasing in east of range

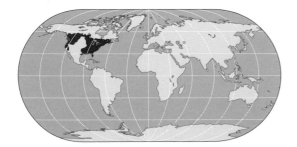

Green Woodpecker

Common name Green woodpecker (Eurasian green woodpecker)

Scientific name *Picus viridis*

Family Picidae

Order Piciformes

Size Length: 12–13 in (30–33 cm); wingspan: 16–16.5 in (41–42 cm); weight: 4.9–8.8 oz (139–249 g)

Key features Olive-green back, contrasting with red crown and black mask; dark "mustache," black on female, black with red center on male; yellow-green rump, pale below; juvenile streaked and barred, with grayish head

Habits Feeds on the ground, occasionally in trees; undulating flight; often calls from treetops; solitary outside breeding season

Nesting Excavates hole in dead or dying tree; 5–8 eggs; incubation 14–17 days; young fledge after 23–27 days; 1 brood

Voice Distinctive, repeated "plue-plue-plue" given with increasing velocity; laughing call

Diet Largely ants; also other insects and fruit

Habitat Open deciduous or mixed forests; also parks, orchards, and heaths in west of range

Distribution Europe, from Britain west into Russia, south to Iberia and north to southern Scandinavia

Status Not yet globally threatened, but declining

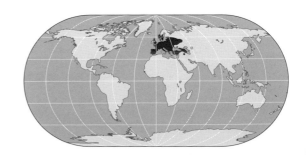

Keel-Billed Toucan

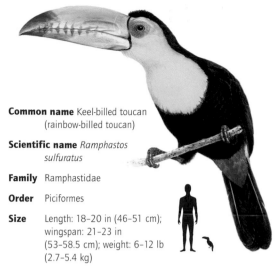

Common name Keel-billed toucan (rainbow-billed toucan)

Scientific name *Ramphastos sulfuratus*

Family Ramphastidae

Order Piciformes

Size Length: 18–20 in (46–51 cm); wingspan: 21–23 in (53–58.5 cm); weight: 6–12 lb (2.7–5.4 kg)

Key features Large toucan with huge, multicolored bill; upper parts and lower underparts black; brownish-maroon crown, hindneck, and upper back; face, throat, and breast yellow, with red band; tail coverts white; undertail coverts red; face skin yellowish-green, blue, or orange; eyes green, yellow, or brown; legs and feet bluish; female has smaller bill

Habits In small groups all year except when nesting, when pairs separate from rest of group

Nesting Natural hole in tree; 1–4 white eggs; incubation period unknown; young fledge after 42–47 days; 1 brood

Voice Various croaking, grunting, and grating notes

Diet Fruits of many different trees, shrubs, and lianas (woody vines); also insects, spiders, eggs, some lizards, snakes, and other small vertebrates

Habitat Mainly mature tropical lowland rain forest, extending into drier areas along streams; in some parts of range also subtropical forest on lower slopes of mountains

Distribution From southeastern Mexico through Central America to northern Colombia and extreme northwestern Venezuela

Status Reasonably common in much of range, but suffering declines in some areas due to deforestation and hunting

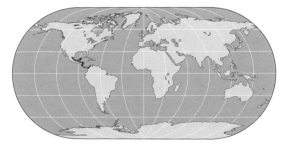

Toucan Barbet

Common name Toucan barbet

Scientific name *Semnornis ramphastinus*

Family Capitonidae

Order Piciformes

Size Length: 7.5–8 in (19–20 cm); wingspan: 10 in (25 cm); weight: 3–4 oz (85–113 g)

Key features Stout-bodied and neckless; big head, short, deep, pale-yellow bill swollen at base, with black band near tip; bright plumage pattern with black crown extending around eyes, black stripe on nape, white stripe behind red eye; back golden brown, rump yellow, sides of head, throat, chest, wings, and tail blue-gray; breast and center of belly red, rest of belly and flanks golden yellow; male has erectile tuft of black feathers on nape

Habits Lives mainly in groups with "helpers" assisting pair in breeding

Nesting Nest hole about 5 ft (1.5 m) up in dead tree; 2–3 white eggs; incubation 14–15 days; young fledge after 43–46 days; usually 1, sometimes 2 or even 3, broods

Voice Both sexes utter song of loud honking notes, often as duet; calls include soft "quock" and squirrel-like scolding sounds; also snaps bill loudly in alarm

Diet Wide variety of fruits; also invertebrates

Habitat Wet mountain forests

Distribution Andes mountains of western Colombia and Ecuador

Status Uncommon or only locally common; listed as Near-threatened

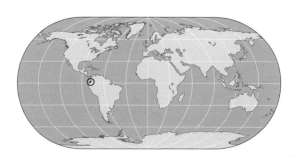

Rock Dove

Common name Rock dove (rock pigeon, feral pigeon, town pigeon)

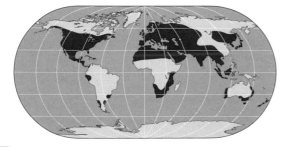

Scientific name *Columba livia*

Family Columbidae

Order Columbiformes

Size Length: 12 in (30 cm); wingspan: 18 in (46 cm); weight: 9 oz (255 g)

Key features Medium-sized pigeon; wild-type birds dark gray on head and tail, paler on wings and lower body, with iridescent green and pink neck patch; feral-type birds very variable, often with checkered or reddish plumage; red eyes and coral-red legs; sexes alike

Habits Highly sociable; wild birds shy, swift-flying; feral birds tame; courting male displays on ground, bowing and ruffling head feathers; also has circular display flight

Nesting All year, in loose colonies; cup nest of stems, leaves, and roots, with no lining, on a ledge; 2 white eggs; incubation 16–19 days, by female only; young fledge after 35–37 days; usually 3 broods in wild

Voice Throaty coo with slight stammer

Diet Wild birds eat mostly grain; feral birds eat all kinds of scraps

Habitat Sea cliffs and inland rock faces; also towns and cities

Distribution Almost worldwide apart from the far north, but scarce in South America

Status Abundant

Common Cuckoo

Common name Common cuckoo (European cuckoo)

Scientific name *Cuculus canorus*

Family Cuculidae

Order Cuculiformes

Size Length: 12–13 in (30.5–33 cm); wingspan: 21.6–23.6 in (55–60 cm); weight: 4 oz (113 g)

Key features Hawklike bird with long, graduated tail, pointed wings, small head; plumage largely gray, with transverse black bars on white breast, white bars on black tail; yellow legs; rare variant female plumage brown; juvenile barred rufous, with white patch on nape

Habits Distinctive flight with shallow beats; secretive, spending much time quietly in trees; most active at dusk and dawn; birds gather at favored feeding areas

Nesting Brood parasite, laying eggs in nests of other birds, mainly insectivorous songbirds; 1 egg per nest, but up to 25 per female per season; incubation 11.5–12.5 days; young evict host's eggs or chicks and fledge after 17–21 days; 1 egg-laying season per year

Voice Male gives far-carrying "cuck-oo" repeated several times; female utters loud trill

Diet Large insects, especially hairy caterpillars and beetles; also birds' eggs and nestlings

Habitat Woodland, marshes, farmland, and heathland

Distribution Throughout Eurasia and northwest tip of Africa; also southern Africa, India, and Southeast Asia

Status Not threatened

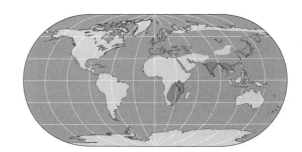

Hoatzin

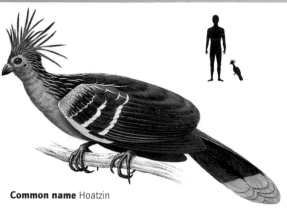

Common name Hoatzin

Scientific name *Opisthocomus hoazin*

Family Opisthocomidae

Order Cuculiformes

Size Length: 24–27.5 in (61–70 cm); wingspan: 37–42 in (94–107 cm); weight: 1.5–2.0 lb (0.7–0.9 kg)

Key features Heavy body; large tail; small head; blue facial skin; red eyes; long, wispy crest; strong legs; upper parts dark brown; head and neck streaked creamy-white; cream breast; russet lower breast, belly, and primaries; chicks have 2 claws on each wing

Habits Clambers clumsily through branches searching for food; loose, weak, mostly gliding flight

Nesting In rainy season; nest a platform of sticks placed in dense tree or bush; 2 eggs, occasionally up to 4; incubation 30–31 days; young fledge after 14–21 days; 1 brood

Voice Noisy, with many different calls such as grunts, croaks, and hisses

Diet Leaves, buds, and flowers

Habitat Trees and bushes beside lowland waterways, including mangroves

Distribution Northern half of South America, especially Amazonia

Status Not threatened

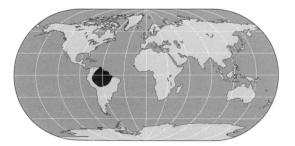

Resplendent Quetzal

Beautiful Bird!

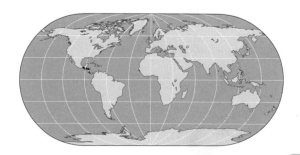

Common name Resplendent quetzal

Scientific name *Pharomachrus mocinno*

Family Trogonidae

Order Trogoniformes

Size Length: 14–15.75 in (36–40 cm), tail streamers of male up to 25.5 in (65 cm) longer; wingspan: 20–24 in (51–61 cm); weight: 6.3–7.4 oz (179–210 g)

Key features Pigeon-sized with big head and eyes, short neck; compact body; short legs; male has iridescent golden-green head, breast, and upper parts; bristly crest covers base of yellow bill; long wing coverts form cape over shoulders; long tail coverts form trailing plume; mainly bright red below; female duller with short tail

Habits Mainly solitary; in pairs in breeding season

Nesting Unlined hole excavated in decaying tree trunk; 1–2 greenish-blue eggs; incubation 17–19 days by both parents; young fledge after 23–31 days; 1–2 broods

Voice Song of male a repeated "k-yoi k-yow"; calls include cackling "waka-waka-waka-waka"

Diet Mainly fruit and seeds; also insects and larvae; some lizards, frogs, and snails

Habitat Breeds in montane cloud forest

Distribution Breeds in highlands of southern Mexico and Central America from Guatemala to western Panama; makes annual migrations to woodlands at lower altitude

Status Near-threatened; increasingly scarce in many areas

Ruby-Throated Hummingbird

Common name Ruby-throated hummingbird

Scientific name *Archilochus colubris*

Family Trochilidae

Order Apodiformes

Size Length: 3.75 in (9.5 cm); wingspan: 4.5 in (11.5 cm); weight: 0.1 oz (2.8 g)

Key features Minute, with long, pointed wings typical of hummingbirds and making soft hum; short, forked tail with spiky tip; long, slender needlelike bill; small head and thin neck; plumage mainly iridescent green, with whitish underparts; male has glittering red throat

Habits Active and pugnacious, usually seen hovering at flowers

Nesting Cup nest of bud scales and lichen, bound with spider silk, usually on horizontal or downward-inclining branch of deciduous tree; 2 white eggs; incubation 16 days by female; young fledge after 15–28 days; 1 brood

Voice Male's song is high-pitched rattle; also "tsip" call during chases

Diet Nectar and insects

Habitat Deciduous and mixed woodland and gardens

Distribution Eastern North America and Central America

Status Common, but may be in decline

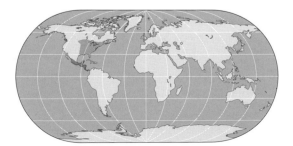

Eurasian Swift

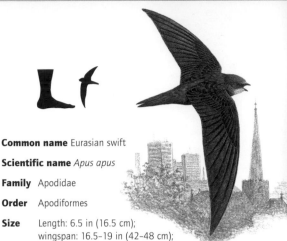

Common name Eurasian swift

Scientific name *Apus apus*

Family Apodidae

Order Apodiformes

Size Length: 6.5 in (16.5 cm); wingspan: 16.5–19 in (42–48 cm); weight: 1.3–1.8 oz (37–51 g)

Key features Large swift with long, curved, sharply pointed wings; deeply forked tail; black-brown with paler upper surfaces to flight feathers; off-white chin and throat; juvenile darker with larger throat patch

Habits Strictly aerial except when on nest; hunts by day

Nesting Normally in small colony in roof space of building, hollow tree, or crevice; usually 2–3 eggs (rarely 1–4); incubation 18–27 days; young fledge after 37–56 days depending on food supply dictated by weather; 1 brood

Voice Shrill scream in flight; rapid chirruping at nest

Diet Small flying insects and airborne spiders

Habitat The air over all types of terrain from forests to semideserts; often over towns and cities

Distribution Europe and Asia, from Ireland east to northern China and from northern Scandinavia south to northern Africa, Iran, and sub-Saharan Africa

Status Increasing in some parts of Europe, possibly declining in others; not globally threatened

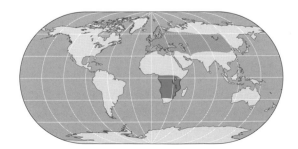

Whippoorwill

Common name Whippoorwill

Scientific name *Caprimulgus vociferus*

Family Caprimulgidae

Order Caprimulgiformes

Size Length: 8.5–10.5 in (21.5–27 cm); wingspan: 18–19.5 in (46–49.5 cm); weight: 1.5–2.5 oz (43–71 g)

Key features Medium-sized nightjar with short legs; small bill; big, dark eyes; cryptic plumage grayish brown above; buff cheeks; underparts brown, spotted and barred pale gray-and-buff; male has pale-gray breast band and broad white tips to outer tail feathers; female has narrow buff tips; immature similar but with more buff

Habits Aerial insect hunter; active at night and twilight

Nesting On ground in clearing, in leaf litter, often beneath undergrowth; 1–2 eggs; incubation 19–21 days; young fledge after 15 days; often 2 broods

Voice Male gives repeated, whistling "whip, poor-will"; also short, sharp "quit" and variety of coos, chuckles, and hisses

Diet Mainly flying insects

Habitat Forest, woodland, suburban gardens, scrub

Distribution Central and southeastern Canada, central, eastern, and southwestern U.S., Mexico, and Central America south to Nicaragua

Status Common over much of range, but declining in eastern U.S. owing to loss of wild habitat, pesticide pollution, roadkill, and predation by domestic cats

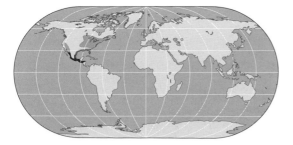

European Bee-Eater

Common name European bee-eater (bee-eater, Eurasian bee-eater)

Scientific name *Merops apiaster*

Family Meropidae

Order Coraciiformes

Size Length: 10.5–11.5 in (27–29 cm); wingspan: 17–19 in (43–48 cm); weight: 1.7–2.8 oz (48–79 g)

Key features Slender body; long central tail spike; black mask and bill; chestnut-brown above with golden-yellow shoulder patch and green tail; underside turquoise-blue, with yellow, black-edged throat patch; silvery-copper underwing with black trailing edge; sexes alike

Habits Social, often perching in small flocks on trees or wires; catches insects in flight or by dropping to ground; very vocal

Nesting In hole in cliff or bank, in unlined chamber at end of tunnel; 6–7 eggs; incubation 20 days; young fledge after 20–25 days; 1 brood

Voice Far-carrying, ringing, but mellow, liquid "prrup" or "quilp"

Diet Bees and wasps, also dragonflies, butterflies, and moths

Habitat Open country with bushy slopes and sandy cliffs; all kinds of farmed land, woodland edge, orchards

Distribution Southern and eastern Europe, Middle East and western Asia, North Africa; also West, East, and southern Africa

Status Locally common

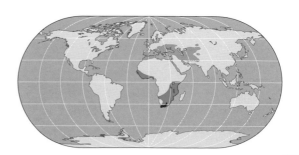

Hoopoe

Common name Hoopoe

Scientific name *Upupa epops*

Family Upupidae

Order Coraciiformes

Size Length: 10–11 in (25–28 cm); wingspan: 16.5–18 in (42–46 cm); weight: 1.4–2.8 oz (40–80 g)

Key features Slender, curved bill; pale sandy-pink plumage, with back, tail, and wings boldly barred black and white; black-tipped, fan-shaped crest; black legs; sexes alike

Habits Feeds on ground, probing for insects; solitary or in small parties

Nesting In thinly lined hole in tree or building; 7–8 eggs; incubation 15–16 days; young fledge after 26–29 days; 1 brood

Voice Soft, musical, quick triple hoot or coo, "poo-poo-pooo"

Diet Large insects, grubs, and other invertebrates such as centipedes, plus small frogs and lizards taken from the ground; also berries

Habitat Open spaces between trees and bushes; sandy ground, orchards, and olive groves; warm, bushy slopes

Distribution Found across southern, Central, and northeast Europe, Middle East, and across Central, southern, and Southeast Asia; Africa north and south of Sahara; Madagascar

Status Common

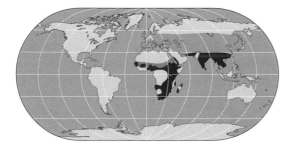

Great Indian Hornbill

Common name Great Indian hornbill, (great pied horn bill, great hornbill)

Scientific name *Buceros bicornis*

Family Bucerotidae

Order Coraciiformes

Size Length: 37–41 in (94–104 cm); wingspan: 58–64 in (145–163 cm); weight: males 5.7–7.5 lb (2.6–3.4 kg), females 4.6–7.3 lb (2.1–3.3 kg)

Key features Large bird with huge yellow-and-black downcurved bill and large concave-topped casque; black face, back, underparts, and wings, with double white wing bar; white neck, upper breast, thighs, and undertail; tail white with broad black band; male has red eyes with black rims; female has smaller bill and casque, and white eyes with red rims

Habits Monogamous; territorial; usually seen in pairs or small groups

Nesting Natural tree hole, female sealed inside it for 4 months; 1–4 (usually 2) white eggs; incubation 38–40 days; young fledge after 72–96 days; 1 brood

Voice Hoarse barks, roars, and grunting sounds; distinctive, reverberating, repeated "tok"

Diet Mainly fruit; large insects and other invertebrates, small reptiles, birds, and mammals, especially to feed young

Habitat Mainly primary evergreen and deciduous rain forest, but will cross open areas to travel between forest patches

Distribution Southwestern India, southern Himalayas, northern Burma, southern China, Vietnam, south to Malay Peninsula and Sumatra

Status Near-threatened; declining in many areas

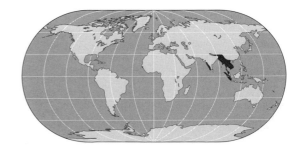

Belted Kingfisher

Common name Belted kingfisher

Scientific name *Megaceryle alcyon*

Family Alcedinidae

Order Coraciiformes

Size Length: 11–13 in (28–33 cm); wingspan: 20–27 in (51–68 cm); weight: 4–6.3 oz (113–178 g)

Key features Thickset with large head and ragged crest; huge, daggerlike beak; gray with white underparts; both sexes have gray chest belt, but female has red band on belly

Habits Spends most time perching, waiting for prey; dives into water for fish

Nesting Digs tunnel holes in banks; usually 6-7 eggs; incubation 24 days; young fledge after 42 days; 1 brood

Voice Loud, rattling calls given by both sexes

Diet Mainly fish, but also opportunistic—feeding on amphibians, insects, small mammals, and birds

Habitat Common around lakes, ponds, rivers, streams, and estuaries

Distribution Found throughout North America; also in Central America, Caribbean, and northern Colombia

Status Not globally threatened; widespread and common in many areas

European Roller

Common name European roller

Scientific name *Coracias garrulus*

Family Coraciidae

Order Coraciiformes

Size Length: 12–12.5 in (30.5–32 cm); wingspan: 20–22 in (51–56 cm); weight: 4.5–5.6 oz (128–159 g)

Key features Large, big-headed, short-necked, stocky crowlike bird with vivid plumage; light-blue head and underparts, rich brown back, ultramarine rump, brilliant green-blue wing coverts, flight feathers black above, violet-blue below; black bill and eye; immature duller, greener

Habits Typically hunts on ground from perch by day; migrates in large flocks

Nesting In unlined hole in large tree, cliff, or sometimes building; usually 4–5 eggs (up to 6) laid May–July; incubation 17–19 days; young fledge after 25–30 days; 1 brood

Voice Harsh, crowlike "rak-rak"

Diet Mainly large insects such as beetles and crickets; also scorpions, spiders, frogs, lizards, voles, and other small animals

Habitat Open forest, well-wooded farmland, and savanna

Distribution Southern, central, and eastern Europe, Southwest Asia, North Africa, and Africa south of the Sahara Desert

Status Declining in northwest but still abundant in eastern Europe and Africa

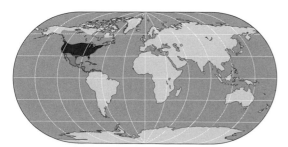

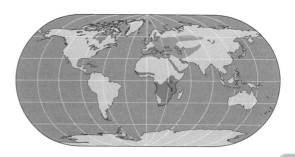

Indian Pitta

Common name Indian pitta (blue-winged pitta, Bengal pitta)

Scientific name *Pitta brachyura*

Family Pittidae

Order Passeriformes

Size Length: 7.5 in (19 cm); wingspan: 16 in (40.6 cm); weight: 1.4–1.8 oz (40–51 g)

Key features Large head, round body, and tiny tail; thick bill and strong, pale legs; black-and-buff striped head, green back, vivid blue on rump and wing coverts; rusty red on belly and under tail

Habits Secretive, skulking on forest floor, dashing off in flurry of color if disturbed

Nesting Untidy globular nest on foundation of sticks, with entrance at one end; foundation often massive if built in tree, but smaller when on ground; 4–5 creamy white eggs; incubation 17 days (captive); young fledge after 15 days; probably 1 brood

Voice Clear, short double whistle, occasionally triple note, mostly at dusk in all seasons

Diet Invertebrates, including many insects, snails, earthworms, and millipedes

Habitat Deeply shaded thickets and deciduous or evergreen forest with dense undergrowth

Distribution India, with isolated population in Pakistan

Status Not uncommon, but much declined in recent decades with loss of forest habitat and trapping of migrants

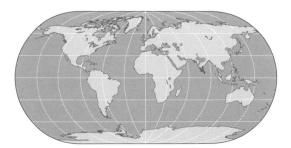

Vermilion Flycatcher

Common name Vermilion flycatcher

Scientific name *Pyrocephalus rubinus*

Family Tyrannidae

Order Passeriformes

Size Length: 6 in (15 cm); wingspan: 14–15.5 in (35.5–39.5 cm); weight: 0.5 oz (14 g)

Key features Wedge-shaped, fan-tailed flycatcher with short legs and small bill; male mainly black-brown above; crown and underside vivid red; female paler brown with dark cheeks and white breast streaked gray-brown; female pale pink on belly in northern birds, whitish or yellow in southern races; juvenile brown above, pale below with dark brown spots

Habits Perches upright on twigs and branches, pumping and fanning its tail; flies out after insects; male rises in fluttery display flight

Nesting Nests in tree fork; 2–4 eggs, white with dark spots; incubation 14–15 days by female; young fledge after 14–16 days; 2 broods

Voice Sharp "tsik" call; male's song is soft, tinkling, repeated "pit-a-see pit-a-see," given while perched, but most persistently in song flights

Diet Insects, including many species of grasshoppers, beetles, flies, and wasps

Habitat Streamside trees in dry or semiarid areas; ranchland and savanna

Distribution From Arizona, New Mexico, and Texas south through Central America to Peru, Brazil, Bolivia, Paraguay, and Argentina; also Galápagos Islands

Status Widespread and fairly common

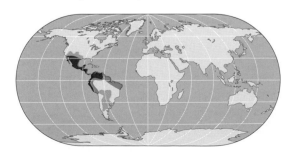

Guianan Cock-of-the-Rock

Common name
Guianan cock-of-the-rock

Scientific name
Rupicola rupicola

Family Cotingidae

Order Passeriformes

Size Length: 10.5–11 in (27–28 cm); wingspan: 18–21 in (46–53 cm); weight: 5–6 oz (142–170 g)

Key features Jay-sized, stout-bodied bird; short tail; short, slightly hooked bill; dish-shaped crest; male brilliant orange, with a maroon band below top of crest; wings mainly blackish; inner flight feathers form long, silky orange filaments; orange-tipped blackish tail, mainly covered by fringes of uppertail coverts; legs orange; female dark olive-brown, tinged with orange on rump and tail; smaller crest

Habits Males assemble regularly to display to each other and to females

Nesting Nest of mud and plant fibers attached to a vertical rock face beneath an overhang or in a cave; 2 pale buff eggs; incubation 27–28 days; young fledge around 40 days; 1 brood

Voice Male gives loud, harsh, catlike miaowing and crowing calls at lek; also squawking, cawing, and crackling sounds

Diet Mainly fruit; also insects and small lizards for the young

Habitat Humid forest, especially near running water and around rocky outcrops

Distribution Patchily distributed in Guyana, Surinam, French Guiana, southern Venezuela, Brazil north of the Amazon, and eastern Colombia

Status Generally uncommon, but can be locally fairly common

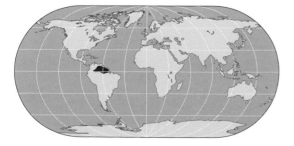

Superb Lyrebird

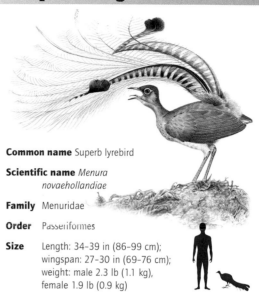

Common name Superb lyrebird

Scientific name *Menura novaehollandiae*

Family Menuridae

Order Passeriformes

Size Length: 34–39 in (86–99 cm); wingspan: 27–30 in (69–76 cm); weight: male 2.3 lb (1.1 kg), female 1.9 lb (0.9 kg)

Key features Dark, long-tailed, pheasantlike bird; plain brown body plumage with coppery wings

Habits Lives singly or in pairs, deep in dense growth but sometimes seen crossing tracks or running along fallen logs; feeds on the ground; roosts high in trees

Nesting Domed nest of sticks on ground or in tree; 1 egg; incubation by female for 42–57 days; young fledge after 43–50 days; 1 brood

Voice High-pitched shriek of alarm; frequent loud, clear "bik" or "bilik"; both sexes sing, male more powerfully, and can mimic with great fidelity; basic song rich and mellow

Diet Insects, worms, spiders, and other invertebrates scratched from soil and leaf litter

Habitat Varied, including dense forest, rocky gullies, plantations, and gardens

Distribution Eastern Australia

Status Scarce, declining locally but introduced into new sites

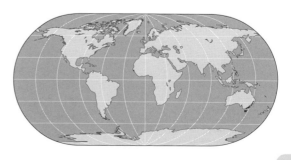

Satin Bowerbird

Common name Satin bowerbird

Scientific name *Ptilonorhynchus violaceus*

Family Ptilonorhynchidae

Order Passeriformes

Size Length: 11–13.4 in (28–34 cm); wingspan: 18.5–21 in (47–53 cm); weight: 5.8–8.4 oz (164–238 g)

Key features Sturdy bird; stout, curved bill; prominent eyes; short tail; strong legs; mature male has glossy blue-black plumage, greenish-yellow bill with blue-gray base, blue eyes, and greenish legs; female dull grayish-green above, with reddish-brown wings and tail, pale yellowish-buff underparts with scaly patterning; dark brown bill, gray-brown legs

Habits Each male typically mates with more than 1 female, building a bower to attract them

Nesting Female builds saucer-shaped nest of sticks lined with leaves in a tree fork or among mistletoe; 1–3 eggs; incubation 21–22 days; young fledge after 20–21 days; 1 brood

Voice Variety of whistles, churring, and other mainly harsh sounds

Diet Mainly fruit; also insects in summer and leaves in winter

Habitat Rain forests, wet eucalypt forests, adjacent woodlands; also visits crops, pastures, orchards, and gardens

Distribution Extreme east of Australia, with main population extending from Victoria through New South Wales to southern Queensland; separate population in northern Queensland

Status Locally common in much of range

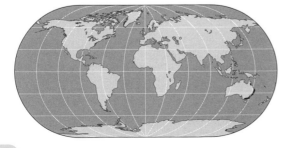

Superb Fairy-Wren

Common name Superb fairy-wren

Scientific name *Malurus cyaneus*

Family Maluridae

Order Passeriformes

Size Length: 5–5.5 in (13–14 cm); wingspan: 5 in (13 cm); weight: 0.4–0.5 oz (11–14 g)

Key features Small wrenlike bird with long cocked tail and long gray legs; male vividly colored with bright blue, blue-black, and black, and mainly brown wings; female and juvenile brown with pale underparts

Habits Moves quickly through dense vegetation in pairs or family parties

Nesting Domed nest of cobwebs, grass, and bark, lined with fur and feathers, usually low in cover; 2–4 eggs; incubation 13–15 days; young fledge after 12 days; 2–3 broods

Voice Repeated "pip" calls accelerate into loud reel

Diet Mainly insects, plus some seeds

Habitat Dense shrubby cover ranging from forests to suburban gardens

Distribution East and southeast Australia

Status Common

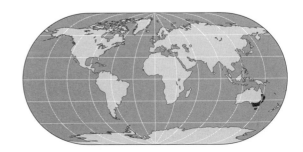

Red-Eyed Vireo

Common name Red-eyed vireo

Scientific name *Vireo olivaceus*

Family Vireonidae

Order Passeriformes

Size Length: 6 in (15 cm); wingspan: 9.5–10.5 in (24–26.6 cm); weight: 0.5–0.8 oz (14–23 g)

Key features Large-headed songbird with wide, flat, faintly hooked bill and red eye; bright olive-green above; gray cap with dark lower edge; broad white stripe over eye; underparts silky white; sexes alike; juvenile has brown eyes

Habits Forages in treetops in dense foliage; calls and sings frequently throughout the day

Nesting Nests in shrub or sapling, 33 ft (10 m) or more above ground; 3–5 eggs; incubation 11–14 days by female; young fledge after 10–12 days; 2 broods

Voice Calls include short, scolding "mew" or "tway"; song is a succession of short, monotonous phrases: "veereo, vireeo, verioo" or "teeduee, tueedoo, tueeedee"

Diet Insects, berries, small fruits

Habitat Woodland, thickets, groves of trees; tropical forest in winter

Distribution North America, except much of western U.S.; south to southeast Brazil and eastern Paraguay

Status Mostly common and stable

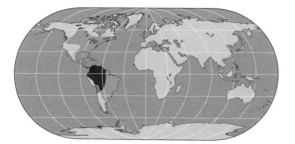

Blue Jay

Common name Blue jay

Scientific name *Cyanocitta cristata*

Family Corvidae

Order Passeriformes

Size Length: 9.5–12 in (24–30 cm); wingspan: 15–16 in (38–41 cm); weight: 2.3–3.8 oz (65–108 g)

Key features Medium-sized, colorful crow, with small crest; blue wings and tail barred with black and white; underparts whitish apart from black "necklace"; black bill and legs

Habits Very bold and noisy; hops rapidly from branch to branch

Nesting Nests made of twigs, moss, grass, and even string in fork or horizontal branch; usually 4–5 eggs; incubation 17–18 days; young fledge after 17–21 days; 1–2 broods

Voice Wide variety of calls, including piercing "jay jay" call and wheedling musical sounds

Diet Fruits, seeds, insects and other invertebrates, small mammals, lizards, nestling birds and eggs, and carrion

Habitat Wooded areas, including forests and parks

Distribution Eastern and central North America

Status Widespread and common; range expanding westward

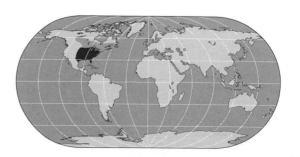

Common Raven

Common name
    Common raven

Scientific name
    Corvus corax

Family Corvidae

Order Passeriformes

Size Length: 23–27 in (58–69 cm); wingspan: 47–59 in (119–150 cm); weight: 2–3.4 lb (0.9–1.6 kg)

Key features Huge, bulky, heavy-billed crow with wedge-shaped tail in flight; all-black plumage, shaggy throat and "trousers"; sexes alike

Habits Glides and soars over open ground or flies with slow, powerful wingbeats

Nesting Builds big stick nest lined with fur and grass on cliff ledge, tree, or building; 3–7 pale bluish-green eggs; incubation 18–21 days by female; young fledge after 6–7 weeks; 1 brood

Voice Harsh croaking calls given by both sexes

Diet Omnivorous, but mainly carrion

Habitat Mainly open wild country remote from centers of human population, including sea cliffs, mountains, steppe, and semidesert

Distribution North America, except southeast; Europe; Asia, except India and Southeast Asia; North Africa

Status Thinly distributed, but very widespread

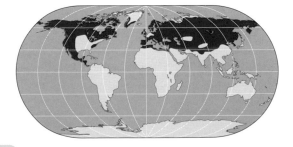

Eurasian Magpie

Common name Eurasian magpie

Scientific name *Pica pica*

Family Corvidae

Order Passeriformes

Size Length: 17–18 in (43–46 cm); wingspan: 20.5–23.5 in (52–60 cm); weight: 6.3–9.7 oz (179–275 g)

Key features Medium-sized crow, with long tail and short, rounded wings; black head, back, rump, and breast; white shoulders and underside; wings black, glossed steely blue, with mainly white tips when spread; tail black, glossed green; sexes alike

Habits Bold and noisy; often forages on ground

Nesting Domed nest of sticks lined with soft materials near crown of tree or shrub; 5–7 eggs; incubation 21–22 days by female; young fledge after 24–30 days; 1 brood

Voice Loud, chattering "chack-chack" calls

Diet Fruits and seeds, invertebrates, small vertebrates, and carrion

Habitat Most habitats where there are a few trees, including urban areas

Distribution Europe, North Africa, and northern Asia, south to Iran, Himalayas, and southern China

Status Widespread and common, although heavily persecuted

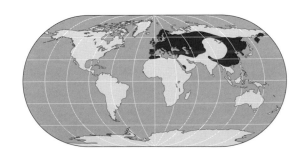

Eurasian Jay

Common name Eurasian jay

Scientific name *Garrulus glandarius*

Family Corvidae

Order Passeriformes

Size Length: 13.5 in (34 cm); wingspan: 20.5–23 in (52–58 cm); weight: 5–6.6 oz (142–187 g)

Key features Stocky, colorful crow; pinkish-brown or gray body, white throat, black stripe resembling a "mustache," and pale, black-streaked crown; black-and-white wings with vivid, barred blue patch; white rump; black tail; sexes alike

Habits Shy feeder; betrays presence by squawking alarm call; flies directly between trees on slow-flapping wings

Nesting Nest of twigs and roots near trunk of tree, lined with a grassy cup; 3–7 eggs, incubation 16–19 days by both sexes; young fledge after 21–22 days; 1 brood

Voice Raucous "kraak" alarm call

Diet Fruits and seeds, invertebrates, small vertebrates, and carrion

Habitat Wooded areas, including forests, parks, and orchards

Distribution Throughout Europe and east through Central Asia to Japan and Taiwan

Status Widespread and common

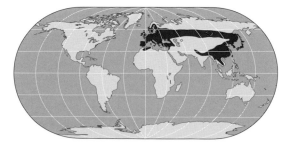

Raggiana Bird of Paradise

Common name Raggiana bird of paradise

Scientific name *Paradisaea raggiana*

Family Paradisaeidae

Order Passeriformes

Size Length: male 13.5 in (34 cm), plus 14–21 in (36–53 cm) elongated flank plumes and central tail feathers in breeding plumage, female 13 in (33 cm); wingspan: 19–25 in (48–63.5 cm); weight: male 8.3–10.5 oz (235–298 g), female 4.8–7.8 oz (136–221 g)

Key features Male's forehead and throat iridescent green surrounded by a yellow shawl; body and wings mainly reddish-brown; breeding plumage has long, lacy, crimson or orange-red flank plumes and a long, wirelike, central pair of tail feathers; female mainly brown, darker beneath, with yellow shawl

Habits Males display communally in trees

Nesting Nest of plant fibers or vines and leaves in fork of a tree lined with softer plant material; 1–2 eggs; incubation 18–20 days; young fledge after 18–20 days; 1 brood

Voice Male song loud, harsh cawing notes; female occasionally gives quiet calls

Diet Mainly fruit; also insects and spiders

Habitat Forest and other wooded habitats

Distribution Southern and eastern Papua New Guinea

Status Common and widespread

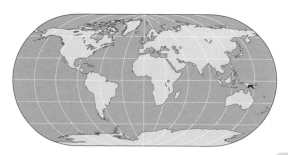

Australian Magpie

Common name Australian magpie

Scientific name *Gymnorhina tibicen*

Family Artamidae

Order Passeriformes

Size Length: 14–17 in (35.5–43 cm); wingspan: 35 in (89 cm); weight: 7.3–13.6 oz (207–386 g)

Key features Strong legs and feet; long, pointed wings; thick, dagger bill; red eye; black-and-white plumage, pattern varying greatly throughout range; juvenile brown-tinged

Habits Feeds mainly on ground, but flies well on direct course; always seen in groups

Nesting Nest a basket of sticks and plant stems placed in canopy of tree; 3–5 eggs; incubation 20 days; young fledge after 28 days; 1 brood

Voice Astonishing flutelike caroling, with tone resembling an organ, carried out in duets or chorus; also crowlike caw

Diet Invertebrates

Habitat Open forest, farmland, suburban areas

Distribution Throughout Australia, plus southern New Guinea; introduced in New Zealand and Fiji

Status Not threatened

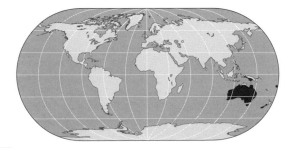

Bohemian Waxwing

Common name Bohemian waxwing (waxwing)

Scientific name *Bombycilla garrulus*

Family Bombycillidae

Order Passeriformes

Size Length: 7 in (18 cm); wingspan: 12.5–14 in (32–36 cm); weight: 1.75–2.6 oz (50–75 g)

Key features Plump bird with back-swept crest; pink-brown with gray rump; black chin; thin, black mask; white wing bars; yellow-and-white edges to primary tips; waxy, red extensions on secondaries (in some birds); yellow tail tip

Habits Appears in flocks in winter to eat berries

Nesting Nest is a bowl of twigs, moss, and grasses in tree, with lining of grasses and lichens; 5–6 gray-blue to blue eggs, spotted with gray and black; incubation 14–15 days by female; young fledge after 14–15 days; 1 brood

Voice Call is a thin, trilling "sirrrr"; song similar; rattles wings when taking off and landing

Diet Insects in breeding season; berries in winter

Habitat Breeds in northern forests, especially in old, lichen-covered conifers; may winter in temperate zones wherever there are suitable berries, including city centers and backyards

Distribution Northern Eurasia and northwest North America, in taiga zone surrounding Arctic, ranging south to more temperate latitudes

Status Probably reasonably secure

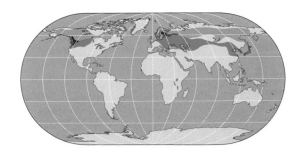

American Dipper

Common name American dipper

Scientific name *Cinclus mexicanus*

Family Cinclidae

Order Passeriformes

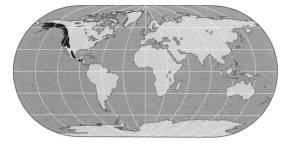

Size Length: 7.5 in (19 cm); wingspan: 10 in (26 cm); weight: 2–3 oz (58–84 g)

Key features Sooty-gray bird; short, dark bill; bulky body with short wings and tail; longish legs for its size; juvenile has lighter bill and underparts

Habits Perches on rocks by mountain streams and rivers, bending legs in "dipping" motion; dives in for food

Nesting Dome-shaped, mossy nest built in early spring, usually on rocky ledge, in tree roots, or under bridges; usually 4–5 eggs; incubation 16 days; young fledge after 23–28 days; sometimes 2 broods

Voice High-pitched, wrenlike song made by both sexes

Diet Mainly aquatic invertebrates and fish

Habitat Mountain streams and rivers, some move to lower altitude waters in winter

Distribution Mountains of western North America, Mexico, and Central America

Status Not globally threatened

European Robin

Common name European robin

Scientific name *Erithacus rubecula*

Family Turdidae

Order Passeriformes

Size Length: 5.5 in (14 cm); wingspan: 8–9 in (20–23 cm); weight: 0.5–0.7 oz (14–20 g)

Key features Small, plump, robust bird with olive-brown upper parts and orange-red forehead, throat, and breast, bordered by grayish-blue band; brown legs and bill; sexes alike

Habits A relatively tame species in Britain, more skulking elsewhere; often dives to ground from low perch to pick up food

Nesting Female builds cup of grass and moss in hollow lined with hair and feathers; 4–6 white or light blue eggs; incubation 12–15 days by female; young fledge after 10–14 days; 2–3 broods

Voice Rich melodic song given throughout year; female also sings outside breeding season while defending feeding territory; calls a sharp "tik," thin "tseee," and high "tswee"

Diet Insects, worms, other invertebrates, seeds, and fruit

Habitat Open woods, parks, and gardens

Distribution From western Europe to Central Asia; north to Arctic and south to North Africa

Status Currently secure

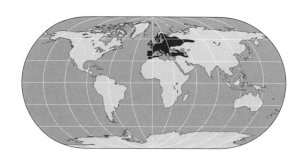

American Robin

Common name American robin

Scientific name *Turdus migratorius*

Family Turdidae

Order Passeriformes

Size Length: 8-9 in (20-23 cm); wingspan: 17 in (43 cm); weight: 2.6 oz (74 g)

Key features Large, long-winged thrush; male has red breast contrasting with gray back and black head; white eye ring; yellow bill; female similar, but paler and duller

Habits Familiar around human habitation, often seen hopping on lawns in search of food

Nesting Cup-shaped nest of coarse grass and mud in fork of tree, manmade sites also used; 3-4 blue eggs; incubation 11-14 days mostly by female; young fledge after 16 days; 2 or 3 broods

Voice Spring song rich sequence of rising and falling notes, described as "cheer-up, cheerily, cheer-up, cheerily"

Diet Invertebrates, fruits, and berries

Habitat Open forest, farmland with scattered trees and bushes, gardens, and parks

Distribution Across North America from Alaska and northern Canada to the southern U.S. and Mexico

Status Increasing

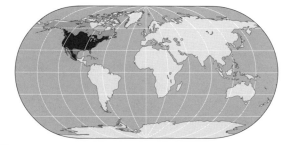

Eastern Bluebird

Common name Eastern bluebird

Scientific name *Sialia sialis*

Family Turdidae

Order Passeriformes

Size Length: 5.5-7 in (14-18 cm); wingspan: 11-13 in (28-33 cm); weight: 1-1.2 oz (28-34 g)

Key features Medium-sized thrush; bright-blue upper parts, red breast, white underparts; male has blue or black wings and tail; female duller and grayer; juvenile brown with blue on wings; brown legs and bill

Habits Often feeds by flying from perch to ground and back

Habitat Grassland with scattered trees and shrubs

Nesting In tree cavity such as a woodpecker hole; 3-6 pale blue eggs; incubation 12-14 days mainly by female; young fledge after 15-20 days; 2 broods

Voice Call described as "chur-lee"; song a development of call, "chur chur chur-lee"

Diet Insects, spiders, and other invertebrates; fruits, berries, and other plant matter

Distribution North America east of the Rocky Mountains from southern Canada south to the Gulf States and northern Central America

Status Not globally threatened

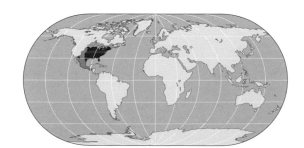

European Starling

Common name European starling

Scientific name *Sturnus vulgaris*

Family Sturnidae

Order Passeriformes

Size Length: 8.5 in (22 cm); wingspan: 14.5–16.5 in (37–42 cm); weight: 2–3 oz (57–85 g)

Key features Strong-legged bird with triangular wings, short tail, and narrow, pointed bill; glossy green-black plumage in summer, with yellow bill; white-spotted in winter, with dark bill; sexes similar; juvenile brown with dark mask

Habits Forms tightly packed flocks, swirling in unison, and noisy mass roosts; feeds on open ground, arriving and leaving suddenly

Nesting Nest a ball of grass and leaves lined with finer grass and feathers in tree hole, cliff cavity, or building; 4–6 eggs; incubation 11–15 days; young fledge after 17–21 days; 2 broods

Voice Medley of whistles, rattles, and screeches

Diet Soil invertebrates, insects, fruits, and seeds

Habitat Open areas and light woodland

Distribution Europe and western Asia; introduced to North America, Australasia, and South Africa.

Status Widespread and common, although declining in western Europe

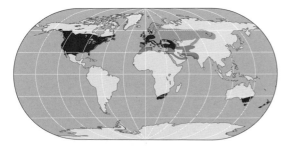

Hill Myna

Common name Hill myna

Scientific name *Gracula religiosa*

Family Sturnidae

Order Passeriformes

Size Length: 11–12 in (28–30 cm); wingspan: 20–21.5 in (51–55 cm); weight: 4.6–5.3 oz (130–150 g)

Key features Medium-sized bird, with chunky head and stout orange bill; glossy black with purple-and-green sheen; white wing patch; yellow wattles on side of face and neck; yellow legs; sexes alike

Habits Largely confined to trees, where it searches for fruit; often seen calling from exposed dead branches at treetops

Nesting Tree-hole nest made of twigs, leaves, and feathers; 2–3 eggs; incubation 13–17 days; young fledge after 25–28 days; 2–3 broods

Voice Range of whistles, creaks, and groans in wild; excellent mimic in captivity

Diet Mainly fruit; also nectar and insects

Habitat Humid forest

Distribution Northeastern India, Indochina, Thailand, Malaysia, Indonesia, east to Philippines

Status Common, but some declines, probably caused by trapping

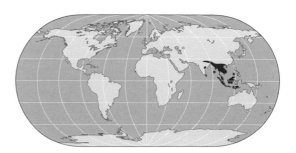

Northern Mockingbird

Common name Northern mockingbird

Scientific name *Mimus polyglottos*

Family Mimidae

Order Passeriformes

Size Length: 8.5-10 in (22-25.4 cm); wingspan: 12.5-14 in (32-36 cm); weight: 1.6-1.8 oz (45-51 g)

Key features Medium-sized, long-tailed bird; gray above, paler below; long, black tail with white outer feathers; wings mostly black with white wing flash; sexes alike; juvenile speckled below

Habits Often feeds on lawns; vigorous defender of territory and food sources

Nesting Builds twig cup nest with lining of finer material; 3-5 blue-gray or green-white eggs, spotted and blotched with brown; incubation 12-13 days by female; young fledge after 12 days; 2-3, sometimes 4, overlapping broods

Voice Complex song includes original phrases and much mimicry of other species; repertoire may include 45-200 song types

Diet Fruit, insects, worms, occasionally small lizards

Habitat Parks, thickets, woodland edges, suburbs

Distribution Southern Canada; whole of mainland U.S.; most of Mexico except south; Caribbean

Status Common; numbers declining at south of U.S. range, but range expanding to north

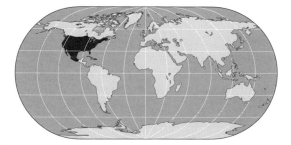

Common Treecreeper

Common name Common treecreeper (treecreeper, Eurasian treecreeper)

Scientific name *Certhia familiaris*

Family Certhiidae

Order Passeriformes

Size Length: 5 in (12.7 cm); wingspan: 7-8.5 in (17.8-21.6 cm); weight: 0.3-0.4 oz (8.5-11.3 g)

Key features Slender-bodied bird with fine, curved pale bill and slim, pointed tail; mottled brown above with pale stripe over eye; silky white below; brown rump and tail; sexes alike; juvenile duller, grayer

Habits Keeps mostly to main trunks and branches of trees, shuffling upward with its body pressed close against the bark

Nesting Nests in tree crevice, building flattened cup of moss, grass, and hair on twig foundation; 5-6 eggs; incubation 12-20 days by female; young fledge after 14-16 days; 1-2 broods

Voice Thin, vibrant "srreeee"; song musical, sharp, rhythmic phrase with flourish at the end

Diet Insects, spiders, eggs, and larvae; pine seeds

Habitat Broadleaved and coniferous woodland with thick, upright boughs and trunks with exposed bark

Distribution West and Central Europe, southern Scandinavia, east across Asia to Japan

Status Stable and secure, common in suitable habitat

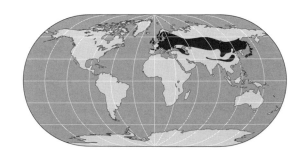

Winter Wren

Common name Winter wren
(northern wren,
common wren, wren)

Scientific name *Troglodytes troglodytes*

Family Troglodytidae

Order Passeriformes

Size Length: 3.5 in (9 cm); wingspan: 5–7 in (13–18 cm);
weight: 0.3–0.5 oz (8.5–14 g)

Key features Tiny, rotund, with short, thin tail, often cocked;
fine bill; warm brown above, buff below, with long
pale stripe over eye; wings barred rufous buff and
brown, flanks barred dark brown; pale pink-brown
legs; sexes alike

Habits Hops and skips through low, dense vegetation and over
rocks; may sing from high in tree

Nesting Builds rounded nest with side entrance under overhang;
5–6 eggs; incubation 14–15 days; young fledge after
16–17 days; 2 broods

Voice Dry, rasping, or chattering "chit," "chiti," and "churrr";
very fast, loud, vibrant musical song includes low,
flat trill

Diet Insects and spiders and their eggs and larvae; also some
aquatic animals and berries

Habitat Undergrowth in woods, gardens, cliff tops, rocky islands

Distribution North America; Asia from Japan and China
westward to Europe and south to northwest India;
North Africa

Status Generally common and stable; suffers occasional big
declines after severe winters

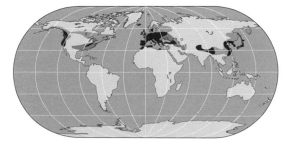

Black-Capped Chickadee

Common name
Black-capped
chickadee

Scientific name *Parus atricapillus*

Family Paridae

Order Passeriformes

Size Length: 5 in (12.7 cm); wingspan: 7–8 in (18–20 cm);
weight: 0.4 oz (11 g)

Key features Black crown and nape, chin, and throat; broad
white cheek patch; upper parts gray-brown with paler
panel along closed wing; underside rusty-buff; short
black bill and gray-black legs; sexes alike

Habits Active, acrobatic, often in mixed flocks; frequently visits
garden feeders

Nesting Nests in hole in tree; 6–8 eggs; incubation 12–13 days
by female; young fledge after 16 days; 1 brood

Voice Typically a buzzy, gurgling "chick-a-dee-dee-dee";
also "day-day-day" and high, clear whistled "phe-be"
or "phe-be-be"

Diet Insects, seeds, berries, spiders, and snails

Habitat Mixed woods, thickets, woodland edges, and
suburban gardens

Distribution North America from Alaska to California and
east to Newfoundland

Status Widespread and common, stable or increasing

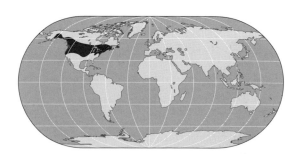

Long-Tailed Tit

Common name Long-tailed tit

Scientific name *Aegithalos caudatus*

Family Aegithalidae

Order Passeriformes

Size Length: 5.5 in (14 cm);
wingspan: 6.5–7.5 in
(16.5–19 cm); weight: 0.3–0.4 oz (8.5–11 g)

Key features Round head and body; long tail; mainly black
wings and tail, shoulders and breast pale rose pink;
white face; tiny black bill; sexes alike; juvenile less pink,
with dark brown face and white crown

Habits Forages restlessly through bushes and trees, usually
in groups of 5 to 15, moving from tree to tree one
at a time

Nesting Enclosed nest decorated with moss and lichen built in
thorny bush; 8–12 eggs; incubation 12–18 days by
female; young fledge after 14–18 days; 1 brood

Voice Calls include short, low "tsup," higher, rippled "tsirrrup,"
and thin "seee-seee-seee"; song is mixture of these notes

Diet Insects, spiders, and their eggs; visits bird feeders to take
seeds and peanut fragments

Habitat Oak, ash, and sycamore woods with bushy undergrowth;
bramble thickets; hedgerows; gardens; conifer woods

Distribution Most of Europe excluding Iceland and northern
Scandinavia, east in a band across Asia to Japan and
northern China; locally Middle East

Status Mostly common and secure; recovers quickly from
declines after cold winters

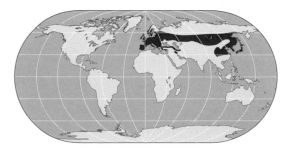

Barn Swallow

Common name Barn swallow (swallow)

Scientific name *Hirundo rustica*

Family Hirundinidae

Order Passeriformes

Size Length: 6.7–7.5 in (17–19 cm); wingspan: 12.5–13.7 in
(32–35 cm); weight: 0.6–0.8 oz (17–23 g)

Key features Slim, medium-sized swallow; small bill; long wings
and forked tail, with outer tail feathers elongated into
streamers; shiny metallic blue-black above, pale to
reddish buff below with blue-black chest band and
chestnut forehead and throat; sexes similar; female has
shorter tail streamers; juvenile duller, with paler
forehead and throat, and short tail streamers

Habits Hunts in the air by day, mostly at low level, often over
water, with graceful swooping flight; often perches on
overhead wires

Nesting Open, featherlined cup of mud and dry grass on ledge,
usually in outbuilding or beneath bridge, sometimes in
cave or tree; 4–6 eggs; incubation 11–19 days; chicks
fledge in 18–23 days; 2–3 broods

Voice Song a melodious, twittering warble; call a sharp
"tswit tswit"

Diet Flying insects, particularly large flies such as blowflies,
horseflies, and hoverflies

Habitat Open country, especially grassland, pasture, and
marsh grazed by large animals, with suitable
buildings for nesting

Distribution Temperate Eurasia and North America, Africa,
Central and South America

Status Common but declining in north due to loss of
breeding sites, feeding habitat, and prey

Skylark

Common name Skylark

Scientific name *Alauda arvensis*

Family Alaudidae

Order Passeriformes

Size Length: 7–7.5 in (18–19 cm); wingspan: 12–14 in (30–35.6 cm); weight: 1–1.8 oz (28–51 g)

Key features Streaky brown above, off-white below, with streaking on breast and flanks; whitish stripe through and above eye; white outer tail feathers and whitish wing trailing edge; crest on crown, which male can raise

Habits Distinctive song and song flight; often found in flocks outside the breeding season

Nesting In shallow depression in soil lined with grass; 3–5 eggs; incubation 11 days; young fledge after 18–20 days but leave nest after only 8–10 days; up to 4 broods

Voice Male's song loud, melodic, protracted stream of trills and warbles in song flight; calls including two-syllable "chirrup"

Diet Plant and animal material; insects important during summer

Habitat Open areas, normally grasslands, cereal farmland; also golf courses, airfields, sand dunes, and uplands

Distribution Europe and Asia east to Kamchatka and Japan; ranges south to North Africa and Middle East; introduced to southern Australia, Tasmania, New Zealand, and Vancouver Island

Status Common but declining in much of its northern and western European range

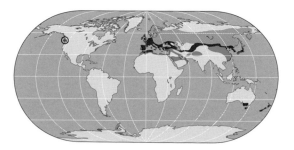

Horned Lark

Common name Horned lark (shore lark)

Scientific name *Eremophila alpestris*

Family Alaudidae

Order Passeriformes

Size Length: 6–8 in (15–20 cm); wingspan: 12–14 in (30–35 cm); weight: 1–1.5 oz (28–42.5 g)

Key features Sleek, long-bodied lark; brownish above, with pale underparts; black band around front of neck; bold facial pattern of black, white, and pale yellow; breeding male has small, black feather tufts (horns) on head; female paler with smaller "horns"

Habits Feeds unobtrusively on ground; forms flocks in winter, often with other species

Nesting Female builds nest from grasses and roots, lined with fur, feathers, and rootlets; 2–5 eggs; incubation 11 days by female; young fledge after 9–12 days; 1–3 broods

Voice Call a short, piping "tseeep"; song a tinkling warble, usually from ground, sometimes in song flight

Diet Adults eat weed and grass seeds; young eat mostly insects

Habitat Tundra, steppes, shortgrass prairies, deserts, farmland, and grasslands from sea level to 13,125 ft (4,000 m)

Distribution From high latitudes around most of the Arctic to northern Mexico, Turkey, the Middle East, Central Asia, China, and Mongolia; also Morocco and Colombia

Status Possibly one of the world's commonest birds

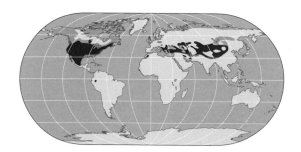

Gouldian Finch

Common name Gouldian finch

Scientific name *Erythrura gouldiae*

Family Estrildidae

Order Passeriformes

Size Length: 5.5 in (14 cm); wingspan: 5.5 in (14 cm); weight: 0.4–0.5 oz (11–14 g)

Key features Small, slim songbird; thick, ivory-colored bill with reddish tip; relatively small head; long tail with pinlike end; bright green upper parts, lilac-and-yellow breast, black-and-turquoise tail; head color varies; sexes alike; juvenile drab brown

Habits Sociable, breeding in small colonies and gathering in flocks outside breeding season; nervous, retreating to treetops if disturbed; feeds by clinging to stems of grasses and similar plants

Nesting Nest a rudimentary bundle of grass in hollow of termite nest or tree; 4–8 white eggs; incubation 12–13 days by both parents; young fledge after 21 days; 2–3 broods

Voice Song formed of hisses, clicks, and whines; main call a thin "ssitt"

Diet Seeds and insects

Habitat Open woodland and grassland

Distribution Northern Australia

Status Endangered, subject to severe long-term decline

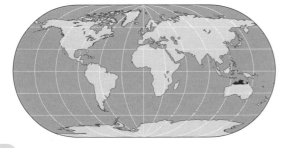

Java Sparrow

Common name Java sparrow (ricebird)

Scientific name *Padda oryzivora*

Family Estrildidae

Order Passeriformes

Size Length: 6 in (15 cm); wingspan: 8.5 in (21.5 cm); weight: 0.5 oz (14 g)

Key features Plump songbird; large head and massive red bill; adult has velvety gray body except for mauve belly; black head, except for bold white cheek; red eye ring; pink feet; juvenile is dull brown version of adult

Habits Sociable, feeds on ground and stems; forms flocks outside breeding season; groups clump together in physical contact, with some mutual preening

Nesting Season varies; nest a ball of grass stems with side entrance; 4–6 white eggs; incubation 13–14 days by both sexes (captive data); young fledge after 3–4 weeks (captive data); probably several broods in wild

Voice Song varies, but typically begins with bell-like notes, followed by a trill and drawn-out whistle; contact call is short, liquid "t'luk"

Diet Mainly rice; also other seeds; possibly small fruits and insects

Habitat Cultivated areas, grassland, and open woodland

Distribution Java, Bali; introduced into many areas

Status Not threatened; common in many places; very popular cage bird

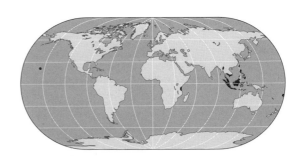

House Sparrow

Common name House sparrow

Scientific name *Passer domesticus*

Family Ploceidae

Order Passeriformes

Size Length: 6.25 in (16 cm); wingspan: 9.5 in (24 cm); weight: 1 oz (28 g)

Key features Small songbird with thick, conical seed-eater's bill; streaky-brown above, plain below; male has bold black markings around eye, on chin, and on breast; also has gray crown, chestnut nape; female lacks all bold coloration; juveniles similar

Habits Bold, noisy, and sociable throughout year; young birds form large roosts

Nesting Season varies; in small colonies, often in thick bush; dome-shaped nest formed of grass lined with feathers; 3–6 eggs, whitish with speckles; incubation 11–14 days; young fledge after 14–16 days; 2–3 broods

Voice Variety of perky chirps; song of male is a series of single chirps in sequence

Diet Mainly seeds, but takes insects in breeding season; urban birds take household scraps

Habitat Essentially wherever there are people: cities, towns, villages, and farms

Distribution Europe and Asia; introduced to many other parts of the world, including North America

Status Not threatened, but recent decline; still abundant in many places

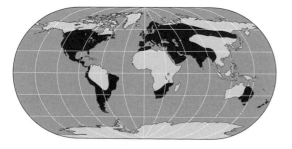

Chaffinch

Common name Chaffinch

Scientific name *Fringilla coelebs*

Family Fringillidae

Order Passeriformes

Size Length: 5.7 in (14.5 cm); wingspan: 9.5–11 in (24–28 cm);weight: 0.7–0.8 oz (20–23 g)

Key features Small songbird with slim body; fairly long wings and tail; rounded head with slight crest; small conical bill; breeding male has bluish crown and pink underparts; female and immature mostly mousy-brown; both sexes have white wing bars

Habits Active and often very tame; common around farms and gardens; feeds on ground or gleans from foliage

Nesting Neat cup nest in tree fork or bush, of moss, lichen, and fibers bound with spider silk; lined with hair and feathers; 4–5 eggs (rarely up to 8), pale blue with dark spots; incubation 11–13 days; young fledge after 12–15 days; often 2 broods

Voice Song is cheerful trill, steadily accelerating and ending in flourish; various calls include far-carrying "pink-pink"

Diet Seeds, plus insects in breeding season

Habitat Mostly woodland; also parks and gardens; often on fields in winter

Distribution Europe east to Central Asia; North Africa

Status Not threatened; one of Europe's most abundant birds

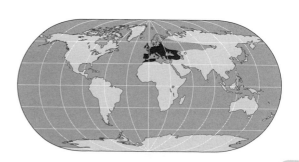

American Goldfinch

Common name American goldfinch

Scientific name *Carduelis tristis*

Family Fringillidae

Order Passeriformes

Size Length: 5 in (13 cm); wingspan: 9 in (23 cm); weight: 0.5 oz (14 g)

Key features Small songbird with small conical bill; fairly long wings and short tail; male colorful in breeding season, mainly bright yellow with black forehead, wings, and tail; females, immatures, and nonbreeding males mainly gray-brown with yellow wash and black wings with pale wing bars

Habits Highly active, with distinctive light, airy flight; feeds acrobatically on seed heads; forms twittering flocks

Nesting Cup nest lined with plant down woven tightly to fork in branch of tree; 4–6 pale blue eggs; incubation 10–12 days; young fledge after 11–17 days; 1–2 broods

Voice Song is lively musical repetition of trills and twitters; call is very thin "twee"

Diet Seeds; some fruit

Habitat Weedy fields and open woodland

Distribution North America north to southern Canada and south to Mexico

Status Not threatened; common, although some declines in east of range

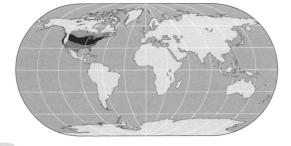

Snow Bunting

Common name Snow bunting

Scientific name *Plectrophenax nivalis*

Family Emberizidae

Order Passeriformes

Size Length: 6.8 in (17 cm); wingspan: 13 in (33–38 cm); weight: 1.5 oz (42.5 g)

Key features Plump songbird with long, broad wings and medium-length tail; typical seed-eater's conical bill; breeding male has all-white head and underparts, black back, and pied (blotches of two or more colors) wings and tail; females and nonbreeding birds are curry-brown and white, with black streaking

Habits Quite tame; often travels in flocks, especially in winter; flocks move forward in "leapfrog" style, birds at the back flying over and in front of lead birds

Nesting On ground; large open cup nest of moss and grass, lined with feathers; 3–5 eggs, sometimes more, pale blue with red spots; incubation 10–15 days by female only; young fledge after 8 days; 1 brood

Voice Song is short, crystal-clear "turee-turee-turee-turitui"; flight/contact call is short trill

Diet Seeds and some insects

Habitat Barren areas of high Arctic, often near snow and ice; also open ground, including fields

Distribution Many parts of Northern Hemisphere

Status Not threatened; often common

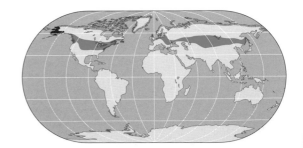

American Redstart

Common name American redstart

Scientific name *Setophaga ruticilla*

Family Parulidae

Order Passeriformes

Size Length: 5–5.5 in (12.7–14 cm); wingspan: 8–9 in (20–23 cm); weight: 0.2–0.4 oz (5.7–11 g)

Key features Male black, paler below, with orange-red on side of breast, in wing, and at side of tail; female greenish on back and bright yellow where male is red; short black bill; black legs

Habits Flits lightly through foliage; catches flies in the air; restless and active

Nesting Male sometimes polygamous; female builds cup nest in tree fork; 3–5 eggs; incubation 11–12 days by female; young fledge after 9 days; 1 brood

Voice Thin "tseet"; wheezy song with slurred, rising flourish

Diet Insects and spiders of many kinds; some seeds and berries

Habitat Scrubby or open woodland; streamside and roadside trees

Distribution North America from southeast Alaska east to Newfoundland, south to Washington, Oregon, Colorado, northeast Texas, coastal Louisiana, and Florida; ranges to West Indies, Central America, and northern South America

Status Widespread and common, but showing recent signs of decline

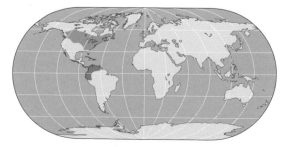

Baltimore Oriole

Common name Baltimore oriole

Scientific name *Icterus galbula*

Family Icteridae

Order Passeriformes

Size Length: 6.5–7.5 in (16.5–19 cm); wingspan: 11–12.5 in (28–32 cm); weight: 1–1.5 oz (28–42.5 g)

Key features Medium-sized, sharp-billed bird; male has black head, neck, and upper back; mostly black wings; orange "shoulders"; black-and-orange tail, orange underparts and rump; female duller, browny-green above, pale orange below

Habits Often lives close to people

Nesting Sacklike nest in outermost branch of tree; 3–6 off-white eggs marked with brown, black, and bluish purple; incubation 11–14 days; young fledge after 11–14 days; 1 brood

Voice Male has loud, melodic song; female has simpler song; "chatter call" used to deter intruders and predators

Diet Insects (especially caterpillars), fruit, and spiders; also nectar in wintering areas

Habitat Deciduous woodland edges, especially near rivers, parkland, shade trees; winter habitats include damp woodlands and plantations

Distribution Most of U.S. east of Rocky Mountains, some of southern Canada, ranging south to Central America and northern South America

Status Apparently stable

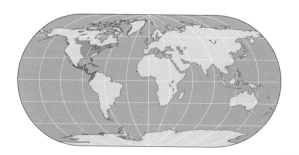

Glossary

Words in SMALL CAPITALS refer to other entries in the glossary.

Alarm call call given to warn others of the presence of a predator

Arboreal associated with or living in the branches of trees or shrubs

Axillary the bird's "armpit"; FEATHERS in this region are called axillaries

Barb side branch from the central shaft of a FEATHER

Barbule side branch from a BARB

Beak See BILL

Bill the two MANDIBLES with which birds gather their food

Brackish slightly salty water

Brood group of young raised simultaneously by a pair (or several) birds

Campo grassland plain in South America

Cap area of single color on top of head, sometimes extending to neck

Carrion dead animal matter used as food by scavengers

Casque bony extension of the upper MANDIBLE

CITES Convention on International Trade in Endangered Species. Restricts international trade by licensing controls. Rare animals and plants are listed in Appendices: I—endangered and most restricted trade; II—not endangered but could be if trade not restricted; III—least restricted trade

Class a taxonomic level; all birds belong to the class Aves; the main levels of taxonomy (in descending order) are: phylum, class, ORDER, FAMILY, GENUS, SPECIES

Cloud forest MONTANE forest in TROPICAL or SUBTROPICAL areas with frequent low cloud cover

Clutch the eggs laid in one breeding attempt

Colony group of animals gathered together for breeding

Comb fleshy protuberance on the top of a bird's head

Communal breeder SPECIES in which more than the two birds of a pair help raise the young

Contour feather FEATHER with largely firm and flat vanes

Coverts smaller FEATHERS that cover the WINGS and overlie the base of the large FLIGHT FEATHERS

Covey collective name for groups of birds, usually game birds

Crèche gathering of young birds, especially penguins and flamingos

Crepuscular active at twilight

Crown See CAP

Cryptic camouflaged, difficult to see

Decurved curved downward

Diurnal active during the day

Down insulating FEATHERS with or without a small shaft and with long, fluffy BARBS; the first feather coat of chicks; in adults down forms a layer beneath the main FEATHERS

Eclipse plumage drab, camouflaging femalelike PLUMAGE acquired by males after a molt in the fall

Endangered species a SPECIES whose population has fallen to such a low level that it is at risk of extinction

Family either a group of closely related SPECIES (e.g., penguins) or a pair of birds and their offspring

Feather unique structure found only in the PLUMAGE of birds; a typical body (CONTOUR), wing, or tail feather consists of a central shaft and a vane bearing BARBS, each with many BARBULES; the lower, bare end of the shaft, inserted in the skin, is called the quill

Fledge to grow FEATHERS; also refers to the moment of flying at the end of the NESTING PERIOD when young birds are almost completely feathered

Fledging period time from HATCHING to FLEDGING

Fledgling a recently FLEDGED young bird

Flight feathers large WING FEATHERS composed of PRIMARY FEATHERS and SECONDARY FEATHERS

Genus (pl. genera) group of closely related SPECIES. See CLASS

Gular pouch extension of the fleshy area of the lower jaw and throat

Habitat where an animal or plant lives

Hatching emergence of a chick from its egg

Hatchling young bird recently emerged from the egg

Hen general term to describe a female bird

Immature a bird that has not acquired its mature PLUMAGE

IUCN International Union for the Conservation of Nature, assigns animals and plants to internationally agreed categories of rarity. (See table below right.)

Juvenile young bird that has not reached breeding age

Lek display ground where two or more male birds gather together to attract females

Mallee scrub small, scrubby eucalyptus that covers large area of dryish country in Australia

Mandible one of the jaws of a bird

Montane pertaining to mountains or SPECIES that live in mountains

Muskeg a mossy bog in northern North America

Nape area at the back of the neck

Nesting period time from HATCHING to flying. See FLEDGE

Nestling a young bird in the nest

Nomadic wandering animal that has no fixed home

Omnivore animal that eats a wide variety of foods from meat to plants

Opportunistic animal that varies its diet according to what is available

Order level of taxonomic ranking

Pampas grassy plains (found in South America)

Passerine strictly "sparrowlike," but normally used as a shortened form of Passeriformes, the largest ORDER of birds

Plumage all the FEATHERS and DOWN that cover a bird

Prairie North American STEPPE grassland between 30° N and 55° N

Primary feather one of the large FEATHERS of the outer WING. (See SECONDARY FEATHER)

Race See SUBSPECIES

Rain forest TROPICAL and SUBTROPICAL forest that has abundant and year-round rainfall; typically it is SPECIES-rich and diverse

Range geographical area over which an organism is distributed

Raptor a bird of prey, usually one belonging to the ORDER Falconiformes

Ruff fringe of feathers located around the neck of a bird

Rufous reddish in color

Savanna term loosely used to describe open grasslands with scattered trees and bushes, usually in warm areas

Scrub vegetation dominated by shrubs; naturally occurs most often on the arid side of forest or grassland, but often created by humans as a result of deforestation

Secondary feather one of the large FLIGHT FEATHERS on the inner WING

Semiarid describes a region or HABITAT that suffers from lack of water for much of the year, but less dry than a desert

Social living together in COLONIES

Spatulate shaped like a spatula

Species a population or series of populations that interbreed freely, but not with those of other species.

Speculum distinctively colored group of FLIGHT FEATHERS

Spur sharp projection on the leg of some game birds; often more developed in males than females and used in fighting

Further Reading

Steppe open, grassy plains, with few trees or bushes, characterized by low and sporadic rainfall and a wide annual temperature variation

Subadult no longer JUVENILE but not yet fully adult

Subarctic region close to the Arctic circle, or at high altitude, sharing many characteristics of an Arctic environment

Suborder subdivision of an ORDER

Sub-Saharan all parts of Africa lying south of the Sahara Desert

Subspecies subdivision of a SPECIES that is distinguishable from the rest of that species; often called a race

Subtropics area just outside the TROPICS (i.e., at higher latitudes)

Tail streamer elongated tail FEATHER (e.g., as on a swallow, tern, or tropicbird)

Temperate zone zones between latitudes 40° and 60° where the climate is variable or seasonal

Terrestrial living on land

Territorial defending a TERRITORY; in birds the term usually refers to those that exclude others of the same SPECIES from their living area

Territory area that a bird or several birds consider their own and defend against intruders and in which they nest

Throat pouch See GULAR POUCH

Tropics geographical area lying between 22.5° N and 22.5° S

Tundra open grassy or shrub-covered lands of the far north

Wader term sometimes used for "shorebird," including sandpipers, plovers, and related SPECIES

Wattle fleshy protuberance, usually near the base of the BILL

Wetland fresh- or saltwater marshes

Wing the forelimb; the primary means of flight in flying birds, carrying the SECONDARY and PRIMARY FEATHERS (quills) and their smaller COVERTS

Wing patch well-defined area of color or pattern on the WING (usually the upper wing) of a bird

Wingspan measurement from tip to tip of the spread WINGS

Wintering ground area where a migrant bird spends the nonbreeding season

Clements, J. F., *Birds of the World: A Checklist*, Ibis, Vista, CA, 2000.

Elphick, C. et al, *The Sibley Guide to Bird Life and Behavior*, Alfred A. Knopf, New York, NY, 2001.

Enticott, J., and D. Tipling, *Seabirds of the World*, Stackpole Books, Mechanicsburg, PA, 1997.

Hilty, S., *Birds of Tropical America*, Chapters Publishing, Shelburne, VT, 1994.

Howell, S., *Hummingbirds of North America: A Photographic Guide*, Academic Press, New York, NTY, 2001.

Hume, Rob, et al., *World of Animals: Birds* (Vols. 11–20), Grolier, Danbury, CT, 2003.

Johnsgard, P., *North American Owls*, Smithsonian Institution Press, Washington, DC, 2003.

Madge, S., and P. McGowan, *Pheasants, Partridges, and Grouse*, Princeton University Press, Princeton, NJ, 2002.

Monroe, B. L., and C. G. Sibley, *A World Checklist of Birds*, Yale University Press, New Haven, CT, 1993.

Palmer, R. S. (ed.), *Handbook of North American Birds* (Vols. 1–5), Yale University Press, New Haven, CT, 1962-88.

Perrins, C. M., *The New Encyclopedia of Birds*, Facts On File, New York, NY, 2003.

Savage, C., *Eagles of North America*, Greystone Books, Vancouver, Canada, 2000.

Sibley, D., *North American Bird Guide*, Alfred A. Knopf, New York, NY, 2000.

Snow, D. W., and C. M. Perrins, *Birds of the Western Palearctic* (concise edn.), Oxford University Press, Oxford, U.K./New York, NY, 1998.

Wauer, R. H., *The American Robin*, University of Texas Press, Austin, TX, 1999.

Useful Web Sites

http://www.aou.org
Founded in 1883, the American Ornithologists' Union is the oldest and largest organization in the New World devoted to the scientific study of birds.

http://www.audubon.org
Web site of the National Audubon Society covers news, avian science, product reports, and conservation work throughout North America.

http://www.birdlife.net
Web site of the worldwide BirdLife International partnership, linking to partner organizations around the globe and providing information about species.

http://www.birdsource.org/warblers/idguide.html
A Web site detailing American wood warblers.

http://www.bsc-eoc.org/links
"Bird links to the world" leads to Web pages of many countries, detailing sites, species, books, and providing other information on the birds in each region.

http://www.neseabirds.com
Information on the natural history of seabirds and where to find them. Includes hints for novice birders.

http://www.peregrinefund.org
A site containing information on many birds of prey.

http://shorebirdplan.fws.gov
The U. S. Shorebird Conservation Plan, with maps and contacts.

http://www.stri.org
Smithsonian Tropical Research Institute Web site provides details of tropical forest birdlife.

IUCN CATEGORIES

EX Extinct, when there is no reasonable doubt that the last individual of the species has died.

EW Extinct in the Wild, when a species is known only to survive in captivity or as a naturalized population well outside the past range.

CR Critically Endangered, when a species is facing an extremely high risk of extinction in the wild in the immediate future.

EN Endangered, when a species is facing a very high risk of extinction in the wild in the near future.

VU Vulnerable, when a species is facing a high risk of extinction in the wild in the medium-term future.

LR Lower Risk, when a species has been evaluated and does not satisfy the criteria for CR, EN, or VU.

DD Data Deficient, when there is not enough information about a species to assess the risk of extinction.

NE Not Evaluated, species that have not been assessed by the IUCN criteria.

Index